Ghana

Ghana

BY ETTAGALE BLAUER
AND JASON LAURÉ

Enchantment of the World
Second Series

Children's Press®
A Division of Grolier Publishing

NEW YORK   LONDON   HONG KONG   SYDNEY
DANBURY, CONNECTICUT

Frontispiece: Kente cloth

Consultant: Michelle Gilbert, Ph.D. (London), Trinity College, Hartford, Conn.

Please note: All statistics are as up-to-date as possible at the time of publication.

Visit Children's Press on the Internet: http://publishing.grolier.com

Book Production by Herman Adler Design Group

Library of Congress Cataloging-in-Publication Data

Blauer, Ettagale.
    Ghana / by Ettagale Blauer and Jason Lauré.
       p. cm. — (Enchantment of the world. Second series)
    Includes bibliographical references (p.) and index.
    Summary: Describes the history, geography, plants and animals,
economy, language, people, and culture of Ghana, the African country
that freed itself of white colonial rule and became an independent
nation in 1957.
    ISBN 0-516-21053-X
    1. Ghana—Juvenile literature. [1. Ghana.] I. Lauré, Jason.
I. Title. II. Series.
DT510.B56 1999
966.7—dc21
                                           98-45226
                                             CIP
                                           AC

  2 3 4 5 6 7 8 9 10 R 08 07 06 05 04 03 02 01 00

Acknowledgments

We are grateful for the help extended to us by Ellie Schimelman and Asante. To the folks at the bead village at Odumase-Krobo, the people at the Ashanti gold mine, and the many people at the markets of Ghana.

Contents

Cover photo:
A woman in Accra

CHAPTER

 ONE The Black Star of Africa 8

 TWO A Tropical Land 14

 THREE A Look at Nature 26

 FOUR Ghana through Time 32

 FIVE Struggling with Freedom 56

SIX A Land of Resources 66

SEVEN Vibrant Culture 80

EIGHT Living with the Ancestors 98

NINE Rhythms of Life 106

TEN Tradition and Change 116

A painted house

Timeline **128**

Fast Facts **130**

To Find Out More **134**

Index **136**

Kente cloth

The Black Star of Africa

On March 6, 1957, a remarkable event took place in West Africa. The people of the colony known as the Gold Coast broke free of European rule. They had been ruled by the British since 1874. Under a new name, Ghana, the territory became the first black African colony to take its place as an independent, modern nation. The people of Ghana were free to decide how to run their lives, how to take care of their territory, how to manage their economy, and how to use their natural resources. They proudly took their place among the nations of the world.

Opposite: **A political rally in Black Star Square, Accra**

Dancers at Ghana's independence celebration

Asantehene Otumfuo Opuku Ware II wearing a large gold ring. Gold is a symbol of the Asante kingdom.

Ghana had a long struggle to reach that goal. It had to fight against the colonial belief that the people of the Gold Coast were not able to take care of their own affairs. The Europeans who ruled the Gold Coast ignored the people's long history and many vibrant cultures. They saw only its great riches. In the early years of their rule, the British showed no respect for the people's cultures and history. Only after they conquered the Asante, the largest ethnic group in the Gold Coast, did the British decide to turn the country into a show-case. They made the colony into a major exporter of cocoa, gold, and timber. They also built schools and trained the local people to run their own civil service.

Even so, the British still resisted the people's desire for independence. Many of the colony's leaders wound up in prison because they resisted continued British rule.

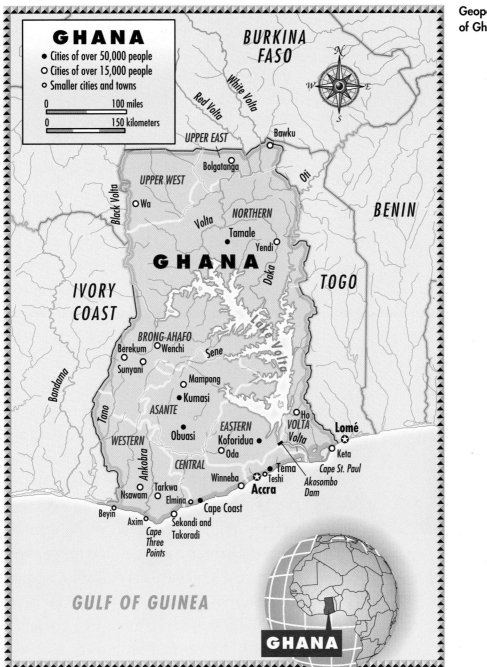

GHANA

- Cities of over 50,000 people
- Cities of over 15,000 people
- Smaller cities and towns

0 — 100 miles
0 — 150 kilometers

BURKINA FASO

White Volta

Red Volta

UPPER EAST

Bawku

Bolgatanga

UPPER WEST

Oti

BENIN

Black Volta

Wa

NORTHERN

Volta

Tamale

Yendi

GHANA

IVORY COAST

Daka

TOGO

Lake Volta

BRONG-AHAFO

Berekum

Wenchi

Sene

Sunyani

Bandama

Mampong

Tano

Kumasi

ASANTE

Ho

VOLTA

EASTERN

Koforidua

Volta

Lomé

Obuasi

Keta

Oda

WESTERN

Cape St. Paul

CENTRAL

Ankobra

Tema

Teshi

Winneba

Akosombo Dam

Nsawam

Tarkwa

Accra

Beyin

Elmina

Cape Coast

Axim

Sekondi and Takoradi

Cape Three Points

GULF OF GUINEA

GHANA

Kwame Nkrumah at the opening of the new Parliament in 1957

Finally, in 1957, Ghana became the first black African country to gain independence. Within five years of Ghana's independence, twenty-five other African nations gained their independence too. But Ghana was the first. It forged the way, with Kwame Nkrumah as its leader.

In order to develop a national desire for freedom, the people in a territory have to feel they are part of a nation. In the case of Ghana, where more than seventy languages are spoken, the sense of belonging to a nation was forged on the battlefields of World War II (1939–1945). The British who ruled Ghana could not have imagined what would happen when they asked the people of Ghana, called Ghanaians, to serve in the British army and fight against the Japanese. The Ghanaians fought bravely for the British, but when the war ended and the Ghanaian troops were sent home, their route took them through India. There, they discovered people very much like themselves, people who were also ruled by Britain. The Indians asked the returning soldiers, "Why are you fighting to preserve British freedom if you are not free yourself?" That simple question would soon find an answer, as those returning soldiers formed the core of the struggle for freedom.

By the time it gained independence, Ghana was as ready as any country could be to rule itself. It had a solid economy based on its rich gold mines and its important crop of cocoa beans, the basic ingredient of chocolate. It also had a long history of culture and knowledge.

Ghana's many cultures and traditions had served its people well. They had strong family ties, and a close attachment to the land they had lived on for generations. The strength of their history and culture made it possible for them to survive the brutal slave trade. Ghana lost many, many people to the slave trade. They had survived this dreadful period when Africans were taken as slaves and shipped off from the coast of this region, never to be seen again by their relatives.

Ghana had a leader ready to guide the country in its first years of independence. He was Kwame Nkrumah, the country's first prime minister. Nkrumah was well educated. He had traveled widely and had studied various political systems. He had fought hard to bring freedom to the 6.7 million people who lived in the territory at that time. There was so much hope, so much that was right, when Ghana became an independent nation.

Cocoa beans spread out to dry outdoors. Cocoa has been an important part of Ghana's economy since colonial days.

A Tropical Land

GHANA LIES ALONG THE PORTION OF WEST AFRICA THAT faces the Atlantic Ocean on its southern shores. It covers an area of 92,107 square miles (238,540 sq km), about the same size as the state of Oregon, and runs about 418 miles (673 km) from north to south. The southern border, where the capital of Accra is located, is 335 miles (539 km) long facing the Gulf of Guinea. The southernmost point of Ghana is just four degrees north of the equator.

Ghana's land borders are formed by three countries. To the west lies the country of Ivory Coast (also known as *Côte d'Ivoire*). The eastern border is shared with the nation of Togo, and Burkina Faso lies to the north and the northwest. Most of Ghana's territory is low-lying. The highest point is Mount Afadjato, just 2,890 feet (881 m). It is part of the Akuapem-Togo Ranges along the Togo border. The lowest point is sea level, all along the coast.

The nation has two main geographical regions—the northern savanna and the southern forestlands. They are divided by a ridge of land that cuts across the country in a diagonal from the south to the northwest. Within these two main regions are

Opposite: **Forests and hills near Ghana's border with Togo**

Mist shrouds this forest near Kumasi

three different zones, each with its own kinds of living conditions. At the coastline, low plains mark the territory. North of the coast lie the Asante Uplands, the Akuapem-Togo Ranges, and the Volta Basin. A region of high plains fills the northern and northwestern sections. Most of the population is concentrated in the southern part of the country.

Moving eastward from the capital city of Accra, the land slopes upward along the coast, gradually forming small ridges and rounded valleys. These gentle hills are well suited for farming, although the low-lying areas become swampy during the rainy season. The continually shifting movement of sand and the temporary appearance of lagoons make traveling in

Ewe children fishing along a coastal lagoon

this region very tricky. Travel by boat requires navigating around unmarked channels and sandbars that change shape as the water rises and recedes. The region is also dangerous for people who live too close to the lagoons. Thousands of houses have been destroyed by flooding and by erosion of the land caused by the ocean waves. The cold, rough surf of the Atlantic Ocean pounds the coastline, making shipping treacherous. For this reason, Ghana has no natural harbors in spite of its long coastline.

The Atlantic Ocean pounds Ghana's shore near Cape Coast.

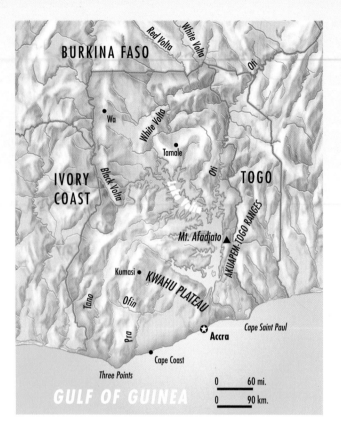

Ghana's Geographical Features

Area: 92,107 square miles (238,540 sq km)

Coastline: 335 miles (539 km)

Highest Elevation: Mount Afadjato, 2,890 feet (881 m)

Lowest Elevation: Sea level

Major River System: Volta

Largest Lakes: Lake Bosumtwi is the largest natural lake; Lake Volta is the largest artificial lake.

Average Annual Precipitation: In the south, 50–83 inches (127–211 cm); in the north, 43–50 inches (109–127 cm)

Natural Hazards: Dry, dusty *harmattan* winds from January to March

North of the coastal region lies the tropical forest zone, occupying about one-third of the total land. The heavy rainfall in this area allows the people to grow many crops, including cocoa and coffee. In addition, farmers here grow basic foods such as plantain, yam, and cocoyam. The Asante, the Akyem, and the Kwawu are some of the people who live in this forest region.

The northern savanna, which covers much of the north, is the driest part of the country. When it rains in the north, it rains all at once, in one season. Then a very dry season follows, with no rain at all. The land here is covered by tall grass and some low trees. These trees store water in their trunks and roots during the rainy season for the dry months. There is one big advantage to the low rainfall: It keeps the area free of the tsetse fly, a deadly insect that kills cattle. This makes the northern area good for raising cattle. This region has the smallest human population.

Ghana is marked by many streams and rivers, although some of these may dry up completely during the dry season or flood during the rainy season. These wide swings in water supply make life difficult for the people who live in these regions, most of whom farm for a living. In spite of these hazards, farmers still work these lands because the silt that forms around the river deltas enriches the soil for crops.

Climate

Ghana's climate is always warm, with average temperatures above 80 degrees Fahrenheit (27°C), and is marked by rainy and dry seasons. These vary from region to region. Some areas receive as much as 83 inches (211 cm) of rain a year while others receive less than 40 inches (101 cm) of rain. Most of the rain falls within one or two seasons, from March to July and from September to November. Some areas have shorter rainy seasons, but the interior has only one rainy season that stretches from April or May until October. Rainfall generally is higher in the south and decreases as one travels north. When the rainy season ends, the land begins to dry up. During the following months, the people go through a period of drought. They must wait for the next rains before the land can be farmed again.

A village on Lake Volta's northern shore

Lake Volta

Lake Volta is a man-made lake and the most prominent geographic feature in Ghana. It is the largest artificial lake, and the largest reservoir, in the world. This unusual body of water sprawls along the eastern part of the country, with branches that look like wide rivers reaching far into the center of the country. The entire lake stretches for 250 miles (402 km) in length, with an average width of 16 miles (26 km). The width is greatest as the lake approaches the Akosombo Gorge.

Looking at Ghana's Cities

Although Kumasi is Ghana's second city in size, after Accra, it is the principal city of the Asante people and the center of Asante life. About 1 million people live in this beautiful city, filled with flowers and plants and located on the Bosumtwi River. Kumasi is the center of both the gold-mining region and the cocoa-growing area, so it is a vital part of Ghana's economy. The city was founded by Asantehene Osei Tutu in 1695. The king named it after the kum tree, a symbol of the Asante victory over the British. The Asante king lives in Kumasi in the luxurious Manhyia Palace. Kumasi's soccer team, Kumasi Asanti Kotoko, has many supporters in this lively city, home to Kumasi University (in photo). People shop in the open-air market at Kejetia, the largest in West Africa. The National Cultural Center in Kumasi includes a museum of Asante history, a library, a craft shop, and an exhibition hall. The average temperature ranges from 86°F (30°C) to 90°F (32°C).

The twin cities of Sekondi and Takoradi are the third largest in Ghana, with a total population of about 300,000. The two cities lie 6 miles (10 km) apart on the coast, about halfway between Accra and the Ivory Coast border. Once a fishing village, Takoradi officially opened as a harbor in 1928. Since then, it has grown to become Ghana's largest port. Sekondi has served as the administrative capital of the Western Region and as an important naval base since colonial times. The average summer temperature in Sekondi-Takoradi is 80°F (27°C); the average winter temperature is 86°F (30°C).

Tema is Ghana's fourth-largest city and its second-largest port. Tema's population has grown rapidly from the early 1960s, when it was about 35,000, to more than 250,000 people today. Tema is a lively fishing port and has a thriving central market area. The average summer temperature is 80°F (27°C); the average winter temperature is 86°F (30°C).

The lake was created in the 1960s when the River Volta was dammed at the gorge. The size and depth of the lake vary according to the seasonal rains. Just after the rainy season, when water runoff is heaviest, the lake achieves its greatest depth and covers the biggest area of land—3,668 square miles (9,499 sq km). The waters of the river flood 210,035 acres (85,000 ha) of land, 7% of all of Ghana's land surface.

The River Volta is actually two rivers. Both begin their journey southward to the Gulf of Guinea from the neighboring country of Burkina Faso. The White Volta travels through the center of the country, while the Black Volta runs along the western border and then turns eastward until it meets up with the White Volta.

Akosombo Dam

The Akosombo Dam and Lake Volta were created in order to use the power of the lake's water to generate electricity. The dam was completed in 1966 at a huge cost to the nation. The building of the dam employed tens of thousands of Ghanaians.

The Akosombo Dam was first dreamed of by an engineer named Albert Kison in 1915 when he discovered a large deposit of bauxite, a mineral used to make aluminum, in the area. He wanted to use electric power from the dam to process the bauxite. But the colonial government felt the project was much too expensive, and Kison's report was shelved for forty years.

When Kwame Nkrumah came to power at the time of Ghana's independence, he ordered that the dam be built. The massive project took more than five years to complete and cost so much that plans to mine the bauxite fell through. The great wall that forms the dam and holds back the waters of Lake Volta stands 408 feet (124 m) high and 1,200 feet (366 m) wide. In most years, it is able to generate enough electricity for all of Ghana.

The Akosombo Dam holds back the waters of Lake Volta.

Before the lands were flooded by the new lake, 84,000 people living in 740 small communities had to be relocated. These people lost their ancestral lands, where they and their families had lived for generations.

Who Has Electricity?

When the rains fail, less electricity is generated from the dam. In 1998, the country's dependence on electricity from Akosombo Dam proved to be disastrous. Electricity had to be rationed. This did not affect life for the majority of Ghanaian villagers, who don't have electricity anyway. Most of the electricity used by individuals and businesses is consumed in Accra, and the biggest single user of electricity in the country is the Valco Aluminum Company. In a typical year, it uses 45 percent of all the electricity produced. Nearly half is used in the rest of Ghana. The rest is sold to neighboring Togo and Benin.

Rivers

In addition to the Black Volta and White Volta, the southern part of Ghana is laced with other rivers. Some are seasonal—they flow when the rains fall and then slowly dry up until the next rainy season. Others flow all year round, fed by water trickling down hillsides. The drier northern region begins at the Kwahu Plateau, near the Akosombo Dam. The plateau stretches across the country in a northwesterly direction. This area has few dependable rivers, making it difficult for the people to find water for household use and for farming.

The most important rivers south of the Kwahu Plateau are the Pra, the Tano, the Ankobra, the Birim, and the Densu. North of the plateau, the main rivers are the Oti, Daka, Pru, Sene, and Afram. Rivers were more important to Ghana's transportation needs before the road and rail systems were built.

This village near Tamale is in Ghana's drier northern region.

A Look at Nature

THE NATURAL RESOURCES OF GHANA REMAIN MUCH AS they were in earlier times, except where forests have been cut down. Several areas have been set aside as wildlife parks and national parks. These include the Owabi Wildlife Sanctuary, Mole National Park, the Gbelle Game Reserve, the Kujani Game Reserve, and Kakum National Park. Other natural areas include Boti Falls, Boabeng Fiema Monkey Sanctuary, and Paga Crocodile Ponds. The Kumasi region includes the Bobiri Forest Reserve, Owabi Bird Sanctuary, and Bomfobiri Wildlife Sanctuary.

Opposite: **A crocodile suns itself on a riverbank.**

An antelope at Mole National Park

Wildlife

Although Ghana does not have huge herds of animals, it has a great variety of wildlife, including elephants, lions, and leopards. Elephants sometimes wander out of the game reserves and eat farmers' crops. There are many species of buck, or antelope, and many kinds of monkeys. Hyenas, jackals, and buffalo also live there. Hippos and crocodiles are found in the rivers.

A chameleon clings to a twig.

A marabou is a type of stork. This one is perched on a treetop in Mole National Park.

Snakes, such as pythons and puff adders, are found throughout Ghana. Two of the most dangerous snakes are the cobra and the black mamba. Other reptiles include chameleons.

Many kinds of birds make their home in Ghana, including parrots, kingfishers, eagles, herons, storks, and egrets. Fish are part of Ghana's wildlife too, ranging from herring, bonitos, and flying fish to sharks.

Plant Life

The kinds of plants and trees that grow in Ghana vary greatly from region to region, depending on the climate. Along the coast, the plants are mainly scrub—a kind of low growth—and tall grass. The baobab tree, a distinctive tree of the region, is sometimes called the upside-

A baobab tree

down tree because of its odd appearance. Its thin branches grow up from the top of its big trunk, looking almost like roots, and it has no leaves most of the year. Anthills are common and may be as tall as 10 feet (3 m). Plants form clumps around the anthills.

In the forest zone, which is found in the southern third of the country, most of the trees are evergreens. There are also tall trees, including the silk cotton tree, the wawa (a kind of hardwood tree), and the African mahogany. Forests once covered about 30,000 square miles (77,694 sq km) of this region, but farming and the timber industry have cut this amount to less than 8,000 square miles (20,718 sq km). The government now requires the loggers to replant trees.

The Ghanaians have turned Kakum National Park into the highlight of their national reserve system. The park is located just 12 miles (20 km) north of Cape Coast. The park and the neighboring Assin Attandanso Game Reserve cover more than 138 square miles (357 sq km) of tropical rain forest. Kakum was declared a forest reserve in 1932, and timber has been taken from it for more than fifty years. The two park areas together were declared a national park in 1992.

This woman works as a park ranger at Kakum National Park.

The park is home to forest elephants, a different species from the elephants found on the plains of East Africa. It also has antelope, monkeys, and more than 200 species of birds and butterflies, as well as many reptiles and amphibians.

The end of logging and the loss of work in the logging industry could have meant a loss of many jobs. Instead, loggers have been retrained to work in the park. The highlight of a visit to Kakum is the aerial walkway, or skywalk.

Skywalk

The best way to see a dense tropical rain forest is from the air. The vegetation is thick and wraps around itself to form a canopy, a kind of umbrella of treetops. At Kakum, visitors cautiously travel along an aerial walkway suspended high above the forest floor. It gives a bird's-eye view of the forest canopy, where many birds and other animals live. It is the only walk of this kind in Africa. The narrow walk is strung 88 feet (27 m) off the ground, suspended from eight enormous trees that are more than 300 years old. It stretches for 1,093 feet (333 m). Wooden platforms attached to each tree allow visitors to stop and observe the life around them.

The aerial walkway at Kakum National Park gives visitors a bird's-eye view of the forest canopy.

Ghana
through Time

T HE HISTORY OF MANY OF THE PEOPLE OF GHANA IS known from two main sources. One is the oral tradition, in which the story of the people and their origins is passed down verbally through the generations. There are people in Ghana today who still keep the tradition and who recite the history of their people on important occasions. The other source of information is archaeological investigation. By studying the tools, fossils, and other traces that people left behind, scientists can tell how they lived, what animals they kept, and what foods they ate.

Archaeologists and historians know that people were living in the region of Ghana as long ago as the early Bronze Age, about 6,000 years ago. They found a home in the lush forests. The area's many rivers and streams provided rich fishing.

Opposite: **An old Asante gold weight**

These scales and weights were used in the gold trade.

Ancient Ghana

Long before the country of Ghana came into being, there was an ancient kingdom called Ghana, founded by the Soninke people. It was located north of present-day Ghana. Much of what we know about this kingdom was recorded by al-Yaqubi, an Arab writer of the ninth century. He described ancient Ghana in detail, writing about its rulers and their gold. He wrote

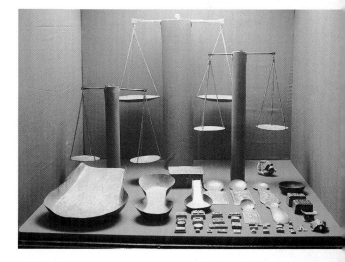

about their courts, in which there were great displays of luxury. The people of ancient Ghana were known as great hunters and warriors. Above all, they controlled the trade in gold. Although the ancient kingdom of Ghana died out in the eleventh century, the name had great symbolic meaning. For that reason, it was chosen as the new name for the country then known as the Gold Coast when it gained its independence in 1957.

Akan Settle in Ghana

Ghana's many ethnic groups tell the stories of their ancestors' migrations into the region. The earliest ancestors of the people who inhabit Ghana today probably began moving into the area about 1,200 years ago. Some archaeologists, however, believe that the ancestors of the Asante people may have been living in the same region for 2,000 years.

The presence of gold, along with the introduction of new food crops into the region, set the stage for larger, permanent populations to form. The Akan-speaking people, living today in the southern part of the country, established themselves at the end of the fifteenth century. At the same time, the Mande people took control of the northern half of Ghana as well as the region that would become Burkina Faso. The Mande, who were Muslims, were active in trading cloth and metal for cola nuts and gold.

Muslims from North Africa played an important role in Ghana. They brought the skills of reading and writing, and they also brought their knowledge of medicine. They were vital to the trade of the region. In this way, Islam, the Muslim religion, became established in the north of Ghana.

Asante People

The most influential of the early kingdoms was that of the Asante, also spelled Ashanti. The Asante are Twi-speaking people who belong to the group known as the Akan people. The state of Asante was powerful, well organized, and aggressive. It attacked its neighbors until they came under its control. By the end of the seventeenth century, the Asante leader Nana Osei Tutu became *Asantehene*, king of the Asante. He organized all the Asante states into an empire and established the Asante capital at Kumasi. It was during his reign that the legend of the Golden Stool began.

The Golden Stool

The chief adviser of Asantehene Nana Osei Tutu was his friend Okomfo Anokye, a respected priest. Anokye created the legend of the Golden Stool. Among the Akan and the Ga people, a stool is a great symbol of power. It is not used as a seat, but to show that a royal person is in command.

The story goes that, one day, the priest brought a wooden stool covered in gold down from the sky. It floated to earth and came to rest on the lap of Osei Tutu. The priest declared that the soul of the Asante nation lived in that stool. It became the most sacred object in the Asante kingdom.

When a new Asantehene takes power, the ceremony is called an *enstoolment*. He does not sit on the Golden Stool. Instead, he is raised and lowered over the stool three times, never touching it. The Golden Stool is taken out of its safe place only on special occasions. To anyone who wonders why the Asante put so much importance on a simple stool, we could ask why a stool should be seen as less powerful a symbol than a crown, a seal, or a cloth flag.

The Asante Empire continued to expand until it began to come into contact with the Fante, the Ga-Adangbe, and the Ewe people to the south. The empire also began to come up against the Europeans who were building fortresses along the coast.

Slavery

The institution of slavery began in ancient times and developed in societies around the world. It was well established in Africa as early as the tenth century A.D. Africans captured in the region of present-day Sudan were part of the trans-Saharan slave trade. Most of these slaves were women, who were used mainly as servants and agricultural workers. Other

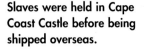
Slaves were held in Cape Coast Castle before being shipped overseas.

slaves from Africa were shipped north to the Mediterranean, where they were sold to Spain, Portugal, and other European countries as servants or laborers.

Slavery was an institution among the people of the Gold Coast long before the first Europeans—the Portuguese—arrived in 1471. Gold Coast slaves were people captured in ongoing ethnic warfare and used as unpaid laborers within the Gold Coast. But the involvement of Europeans in the west African slave trade changed the practice entirely.

The Europeans often claimed they were in Africa to "civilize the natives." However, the practice of shipping human beings across the Atlantic Ocean in chains under horrible conditions showed that they believed in "civilization" for white people only.

Some Ghanaian chiefs and traders were so eager to obtain certain goods that they were willing to sell their fellow Africans to the Europeans. Actually, the term trade is more accurate than selling—the people were traded for goods. Although some slaves were traded for practical items such as cloth, many were traded for guns. With guns, the Africans were better able to defend themselves against other African ethnic groups. With guns, the chiefs saw they could gain more power and capture more slaves.

Many of the Africans sold as slaves did not survive the long, dangerous ocean voyages to North America and South America. The chiefs found that the guns they had wanted so much involved them in bigger and more destructive wars. It was a sad trade.

How Many Were Lost?

No one knows for sure how many Africans were sold and shipped out of Africa as slaves. It is estimated that 10 million Africans were sold into slavery, and that at least a half-million of these left from the Gold Coast. The strongest men and the strongest women were chosen to be sold and shipped away. The slave traders didn't buy old people or sick people. They bought and sold what we would call the best and the brightest—those who had the most to contribute. Those people never had a chance to use their strength and their talents to help their own people. Many believe that the Gold Coast, today's Ghana, never really recovered from this loss.

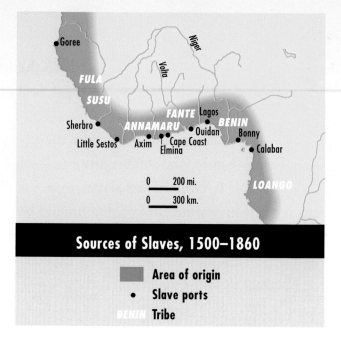

Sources of Slaves, 1500–1860

- Area of origin
- • Slave ports
- BENIN Tribe

Europeans Arrive

The Portuguese were the first Europeans to arrive along the African coast. Their superior navigation skills enabled these great sailors to travel the oceans to regions that were far from their homeland—and to return safely. In 1471, when the first Portuguese arrived on the shores of present-day Ghana, they were rewarded by their king for each length of coast they acquired. They were given the exclusive right to trade in that land.

Wherever they landed, the Portuguese built forts. Originally, the forts were built to create a secure stronghold for the Europeans, who were intruding on the Africans' land. Later, the forts were needed as defense against other Europeans who wanted to take over the same territory. Even today, these fifteenth-century forts are still standing.

Castles and Forts

The first Gold Coast castle, built in 1482, was named *Sao Jorge* (St. George) and is now known as Elmina Castle. *Elmina* is taken from Portuguese words meaning "the mine." The Portuguese saw this region as one big gold mine. But they discovered something even more valuable than gold—the slave trade. For nearly a century, the Portuguese had no competition along the Gold Coast. They made deals with local chiefs who provided them with the slaves. Sometimes the Portuguese captured slaves on their own.

The entrance to the female slave dungeon at Elmina Castle

By the early 1600s, the Portuguese monopoly on the region and on the trade there was challenged by the Dutch, who were also great sailors, and even better traders. The value of the trade was tremendous. The gold mines of the Gold Coast produced as much as 30,000 ounces (850,500 grams) of gold a year for the Portuguese king. In order to buy the gold, the Portuguese bought slaves from the people of Benin and traded them to the Akan, who controlled the gold.

By 1642, however, the Portuguese had lost their grip on the Gold Coast. During the rest of the 1600s and throughout the 1700s, English, Danes, and Swedes sailed along the coast, intent on setting up trade deals with the Africans. Each built forts for protection, and many of these may still be seen. By 1872, the British succeeded in gaining control of all the Dutch forts and became the most powerful European nation on the Gold Coast.

Kingdom of Gold

The first Europeans to land along Ghana's coast, the Portuguese, named it the Gold Coast when they saw gold glittering in the streams. In the same way, the neighboring territory became known as the Ivory Coast. These areas were viewed only as sources of wealth for Europeans, but the people who lived in the region already had their own uses for the

Gold remains a symbol of the Asante kingdom today.

gold. Gold became the symbol of the Asante kingdom, and it was used with a generous hand in the royal ornaments and symbols of kingly office.

The Asante were the most powerful group in the interior of the region. They intended to expand their power all the way to the Atlantic coast. In 1807, the Asante first invaded the coastal area. They wanted to take control of the trade that had developed in gold, timber, and palm oil. They attacked these southern regions again and again in 1811 and 1814, disrupting the lively trade that had grown up over several centuries.

The Asante were very successful in their attacks on the Europeans' forts. The

European powers, united as the African Company of Merchants, signed a treaty of friendship. This agreement extended Asante rule over these coastal regions as well as over the other ethnic groups who lived there, the Fante and the Ga. These coastal people relied on the British for protection but soon found that the British were unable to protect them from the Asante. The British were going to have to resort to force, or give up their growing claim to the region.

Soon the Asante had another problem to face: In 1833, Great Britain outlawed slavery. The British were now firmly opposed to the Asante and the slave trade.

A Colony Takes Shape

In 1830, George Maclean became head of a local council of merchants. He proved to be very successful in keeping the peace and allowing trade to grow rapidly. At the same time, the British began to make treaties with the coastal chiefs, who believed they could use the power of the British against the Asante. A colony was taking shape.

In 1843, Commander H. Worsley Hill was named the first governor of the Gold Coast. British law was spreading along the coast region, now declared a British protectorate. A major change came in 1872 when the British purchased Elmina Castle from the Dutch, ending the Dutch presence. The Asante lost their only trading outlet to the sea.

At the same time, the Fante people, who lived along the central coast region, formed an independent confederation under their own King Ghartey IV of Winneba, a city not far

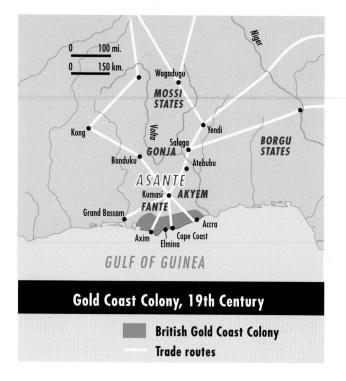

Gold Coast Colony, 19th Century

British Gold Coast Colony
Trade routes

from Accra. This confederation was patterned on the example of modern European states and was viewed with alarm by the British. If the Africans were able to organize and govern themselves in a style so similar to the Europeans, what justification was there any more for the British to hold power? The British acted quickly. In 1874, they declared the confederation to be illegal. Instead of granting more power to the Africans, they declared the Gold Coast to be a British Crown Colony.

Asante

The British had more than just the Fante confederation to deal with. The Asante, with their well-established culture and system of chiefs and kings, resisted British rule with all their might. Kumasi, the Asante capital, was a well-organized city. In the early 1800s, it was visited by a British expedition intent on signing a trade agreement.

The Asante had much to protect. The Asante army was huge, estimated at 200,000

The Asante capital of Kumasi was a well-organized city before the British destroyed it.

men. In 1806, when the Asante attacked the Fante people, the British fought in the battle on the side of the Fante. Skirmishes took place periodically throughout the nineteenth century.

British troops landing on the Gold Coast

General Garnet Wolseley (seated in litter) led the British expedition to Kumasi.

March to Asante

In order to fight the Asante, the British first had to reach their homeland. Led by General Garnet Wolseley, British troops, loaded down with gear, had to make their way through thick forests. They were not used to the intense heat and the humidity. The foliage was so thick that the two sides could hardly see each other until they were actually within combat range. The British, who were used to attacking in wide rows, had no room to spread out. But perhaps one of the worst enemies the British faced was one they could scarcely see—mosquitoes carrying malaria. This dreadful fever killed many in Africa, and it left others too weak to stand and walk.

Although they were greatly outnumbered by the Asante, the British had the best weapons. The firepower of their rifles and cannon was overwhelming. They conquered Kumasi and declared themselves the winners. While they were waiting to get their peace treaty signed, the British looted the city. Much of their loot was in the form of gold. Then they set fire to the city, leveling it.

The Asante kingdom was seriously weakened by this defeat. At the same time, a civil war within Asante itself threatened to destroy the entire culture.

Final Battles

A final attempt to resist the British in 1896 led to the complete defeat of the Asante. The kingdom was at an end, and the Asante became part of the British protectorate. The British left no doubt about who was in charge: They ended the rule of the Asantehene, the traditional Asante king. They sent the Asantehene, Prempeh I, into exile in the Seychelles Islands, far

Asantehene Prempeh I and the Queen Mother submitting to the British army

away in the Indian Ocean. But they did something that the Asante viewed as even more serious than sending their Asantehene away: They tried to find and seize the Golden Stool.

This pushed the Asante into their final war against the British in 1900. Desperately outgunned by the British, they tried every method to resist, including the novel idea of blocking the few paths through the jungle. They dragged enormous logs into place and built barriers, some of them more than 400 yards (366 m) long. They built a stockade on every possible route out of the region. Unlike the British, who had to carry their supplies from the distant coast, the Asante were well stocked with food and water. They also demanded tremendous discipline from their soldiers. The war was devastating to both sides. The British brought in Africans from other parts of their empire, including Nigeria and Kenya, to fight the Asante.

Gold Coast Colony

Finally successful in putting down the Asante in 1901, the British proclaimed the region of Asante to be a colony, ruled by the governor of the Gold Coast. By this time the British had explored farther north beyond the land of the Asante and now claimed the Northern Territories as well. A resident commissioner, under the governor of the Gold Coast, ruled the area. This arrangement continued until 1946.

Asantehene Prempeh II

Prempeh II

In 1924, Prempeh I was allowed to return to Kumasi. Although he still opposed the British, he lived there peacefully until his death in 1931. In 1935, a new Asantehene was named—Nana Osei Agyeman Prempeh. This time the British actually participated in the enstoolment ceremony. For the first time since 1896, the carefully guarded Golden Stool was displayed in public.

By now, the three territories of the Gold Coast—the coast itself, Asante, and the Northern Territories—were united under British rule as the Gold Coast. In 1956, a final piece of land, the Volta region, was added to the colony. Until then, the Volta region had been governed as part of neighboring Togoland.

The British relied on the traditional chiefs to rule over their own people. This reduced conflicts with the British. Concentrating power among local chiefs also allowed the fewest number of people to take part in governing the colony. Limiting the number of people who had access to the decision-making process in this way held the country back in its development. In 1925, the chiefs were formed into provincial councils in the original three regions of the Gold Coast.

Modernizing the Colony

The Gold Coast did enjoy a certain amount of development under British rule. A railroad connecting the coastal centers was built, as were thousands of miles of roads. The cocoa crop was expanded and became a great source of income for the colony. Most of the economic progress was made under Frederick Gordon Guggisberg, governor of the Gold Coast from 1919 to 1927. He set about creating supplies of clean water, sanitation, energy, schools, and all the other services of a modern society. During the early years of the colony, schooling was made more widely available. Secondary schools were established as well as a teachers' training college at Accra. In 1948, the University College was opened.

In the years that followed colonization, the peoples who lived within those political borders began to think of themselves as members of distinct nations, but not the kinds of nations designed by the Europeans. No matter how European their manners and their languages became over time, the black peoples of Africa wanted to direct their own destinies. In a faraway land, the people of the Gold Coast first saw what it was like for a British colony to gain freedom. It happened in India.

Gandhi's Example

The people of the Gold Coast and the people of India were all ruled by the British. During World War II, the British called upon the people in their African colonies to help them fight in Asia. There, African soldiers met Indian soldiers who were also fighting for the British. But the Indians were involved in

West African troops fought for the British in Asia during World War II.

another fight too—the struggle for their own independence. They were very political in their views, and they made the Africans wonder why they were fighting for the British instead of for themselves.

In the Gold Coast, fewer than 5,000 Britons ruled 6.7 million Africans. The Africans decided it was time to get rights for themselves. They began a program called Positive Action. It was based on some of the principles held by Mohandas K. "Mahatma" Gandhi, a leader of India's independence movement. It was an effort to gain independence without having to go to war.

The Ghanaians had their own leader—Kwame Nkrumah—who spoke to the people in a way that they could understand. And he shared another experience with them. When he began to defy the British and urged the Africans to practice civil disobedience, he was imprisoned. (Civil disobedience is the refusal to obey a law on the grounds that it is unjust.) Nkrumah's prison term was a badge of honor in Africa, one shared by most of the African leaders who fought for independence from the colonizers.

British Resistance

At first the British resisted even the smallest attempts toward independence. A march by unarmed ex-servicemen in Accra to present a petition was met by gunfire. The result was rioting and looting, especially of stores belonging to Europeans. Nkrumah was already traveling around the country, talking to people, convincing them that the time was right for them to have their freedom. By 1949, the first important political party had been formed, the Convention People's Party (CPP).

The struggle continued even when Nkrumah was in prison. Komla Gbedema, vice chairman of the CPP, took Nkrumah's place at rallies. So that no one would forget Nkrumah, Gbedema propped up a full-size photograph of Nkrumah at all the rallies and said, "Nkrumah's body is in jail but his spirit is going on." The unrest and the protests continued.

The British could see the writing on the wall. Unless they were willing to commit troops to the Gold Coast to keep the peace, they had to start a process leading to freedom. They already had the example of India, which gained its independence in 1947.

Kwame Nkrumah led Ghana's independence movement.

The First Elections

In 1951, Britain took the first steps toward Gold Coast independence by allowing free elections and a national assembly. There was little doubt as to which group would win. Even though Nkrumah was in prison, he and his CPP won by a landslide. The CPP earned two-thirds of the seats in the new Legislative Assembly, including one for Nkrumah.

The following year, the position of prime minister was created. The prime minister was head of the government of the Gold Coast. The Legislative Assembly elected Nkrumah to this position. In his campaign for self-government, Nkrumah had won the support of the masses of uneducated, poor people. This election was the beginning of the end of British rule. They had no choice but to release Nkrumah from prison.

Independence Day

Changes in the governing of the colony continued over the next six years, with the Africans gaining more and more control. A new Constitution was enacted in 1954. But there was already strife between Nkrumah's party and the new National Liberation Movement (NLM), an Asante-based group.

The British backed Nkrumah's party, and progress continued toward full independence. On March 6, 1957, Gold Coast became the independent country of Ghana. The United States sent Vice President Richard Nixon to the ceremony. U.S. civil rights leader Martin Luther King Jr. also attended.

Vice President Richard Nixon, shown here with Prime Minister Kwame Nkrumah, represented the United States at Ghana's independence ceremony.

Scientific Socialism

The people of Ghana hoped for economic freedom as well as political freedom. To achieve this, Nkrumah decided on a system of central planning, which he called *scientific socialism*. He also took tremendous power for himself. He made changes in the Constitution that ensured only his

Kwame Nkrumah being sworn in as president in 1960. He is wearing Kente cloth.

followers would be in charge of government departments. He kept out the other ethnic groups, including the Ewe people who live in the southeastern part of Ghana. Although they make up about one-fifth of the entire population, in 1961 not one Ewe person had a position in Nkrumah's cabinet.

Nkrumah manipulated elections to be sure they would be decided in his favor. Afterward, he declared that he was backed by the free will of the people. Opponents were jailed. One important opposition leader, Kofi Abrefa Busia, fled to London when Nkrumah declared Busia's United Party to be illegal.

President for Life

Nkrumah believed that his efforts were for the good of the Ghanaian people. He wanted to make rapid economic changes in Ghana and, to do that, he needed to be able to make decisions without any debate. To achieve this, he declared himself president for life and declared that Ghana had only one political party—his own. He banned all ethnic, religious, and regional political parties. These were tragic steps for a country that was meant to be a shining example of freedom. Nkrumah made himself the symbol of Ghana. His picture appeared on everything from women's dresses to the nation's coins. At the same time, he established a network of spies, to catch anyone who opposed his ideas. People could not say anything negative about Nkrumah without facing arrest.

He moved to weaken the power of the traditional chiefs, and, in some cases, he actually removed them from power. This broke a tradition that stretched back a thousand years. Although Ghana had a strong economy based on its exports of gold and cocoa, Nkrumah spent money extravagantly on the Akosombo Dam, aluminum production, and other projects. Overspending, together with government corruption and low world cocoa prices, used up the country's cash reserves. He was forced to borrow money to pay for basic necessities.

Nkrumah's portrait on a shirt worn by Abhasan Brimati, a member of Ghana's Olympic boxing team

A Broader Vision

During his rule, Nkrumah helped found the nonaligned movement, a group of world nations that were not loyal to either the capitalist countries such as the United States or the communist-ruled countries such as the former Soviet Union. He saw Ghana as leader of the African nations still under colonial rule. He proclaimed Ghana the "Black Star of Africa."

The University at Legon in Accra could not take in all the students who wanted a college education, but the country needed many more educated people. Nkrumah began a major plan to upgrade existing schools into universities and to build new schools, including the University of Cape Coast.

In spite of the positive steps he took, many people opposed his rule. But Nkrumah made it impossible for this opposition to be expressed in a democratic way. Instead, it took force to bring about change. On February 24, 1966, while he was on a trip to China, his government was overthrown by the Ghana military. Barely nine years after independence, Nkrumah left behind an economy in ruins and shattered hopes. Nkrumah fled to the West African country of Guinea, where he remained until his death in 1972.

New Leaders

As soon as Nkrumah was overthrown, the opposition leaders were released from prison and Kofi Busia returned to Ghana from England. The new leaders faced a considerable battle. Not only did they have to find a way to get the economy back on its feet, they also had to persuade the people to trust in government.

Spectators at the inauguration of the new government in 1969

This proved to be nearly impossible. For the next fifteen years, the country went into a steep decline, and the people turned more and more to their own cultural leaders.

In August 1969, for the first time since Ghana became independent, there were open elections with more than one political party. Kofi Busia became prime minister but the political troubles continued. And the decisions Busia made in his efforts to get the economy back on track were very hard for the people to take. All they saw was more hardship for them. The debt Nkrumah had left behind was simply enormous. And so it was that on January 13, 1972, Busia was thrown out in a military takeover, called a coup, led by Lieutenant Colonel Ignatius Kutu Acheampong.

Prime Minister Kofi Busia (in suit)

Rocky Road

From 1972 until 1993, Ghana ricocheted from one coup to the next. During most of that time the country was under military rule, which meant that the people did not elect their leaders. Among the people staging these coups was Flight Lieutenant Jerry Rawlings. In 1979, he led a violent but unsuccessful overthrow of the government. He was successful in his second attempt on June 4, 1979. He steppped aside for a civilian leader, Dr. Hilla Limann, who was president from 1979 to 1981.

Flight Lieutenant Jerry Rawlings addressing a crowd in 1981 as chairman of the Provisional National Defense Council

On December 31, 1981, Rawlings overthrew Limann and took over the government. Rawlings held military power until 1992, when he permitted elections to be held. He won those elections and took power as the elected president on January 4, 1993. The opposition parties claimed there was fraud in the presidential elections, so they boycotted the parliamentary elections that followed. As a result, Rawlings's party easily took over the 200-seat parliament.

In 1996, Rawlings was again elected president in open elections. By current Ghana law, he can serve only two terms. He has stated repeatedly that he will step down when his term ends in 2000.

Struggling with Freedom

WHEN GHANA ACHIEVED INDEPENDENCE IN 1957, Kwame Nkrumah had great plans for the country. In fact, he had great plans for Africa. He saw his role as much bigger than just leading this one country. He wanted to erase the lines drawn on the map of Africa by the colonial powers and reunite the cultures that had been divided. There was a strong sense of a new order, a new way of ruling.

Opposite: **President Jerry Rawlings in traditional Ghanaian attire**

Structure of Government

At the time of independence, Ghana modeled its parliament on that of Great Britain. The 1992 Constitution provides for a president, a parliament, a cabinet, a council of state, and an independent judiciary. All Ghanaians who are at least eighteen years old are eligible to vote.

Ghana's parliament building at the time of independence

Kwame Nkrumah

Kwame Nkrumah (1909–1972), Ghana's first president, was born in the village of Nkroful in the southwest region of the colony then known as the Gold Coast. *Kwame*, his first name, is a Fante name given to boys born on Saturday. Nkrumah attended a mission school, where he was an outstanding student and earned a place at a teacher's training college in Accra. He taught for several years before traveling to the United States, where he studied at Lincoln University and the University of Pennsylvania.

Nkrumah spent ten years in the United States, forming the political ideas that brought him back to his home country in 1947. When he returned, he was determined to lead the Gold Coast to independence from Great Britain.

After founding his own political party, Nkrumah traveled throughout the Gold Coast, speaking to packed auditoriums. His program was both simple and bold. He would achieve independence for the people of the Gold Coast, create a democratic government, and help others in West Africa to achieve their own independence. The British jailed him repeatedly for leading boycotts, strikes, and other nonviolent protests.

Nkrumah believed that Africans would gain power by ignoring the country borders drawn by Europeans. These borders often divided ethnic groups between countries. He wanted Africans to work for the good of all Africa. He called this the Pan-African movement, meaning "all across Africa." It was expressed by the saying, "Africa belongs only to the Africans."

Parliament in session

Ghana's legal system is based on three forms: Ghanaian common law, traditional law, and the 1992 Constitution. There is a Supreme Court, as well as a Court of Appeal and a High Court of Justice. Laws are applied at the local level by district courts, traditional courts, and local courts. The country tries to balance the different ways of life in Ghana under the law. In certain situations, this means applying traditional laws, using the system of chiefs.

To carry out the laws, the country is divided into ten administrative regions, and these are divided into 110 districts. Each district is divided further into town councils, zone councils, and so on, until they reach the level of unit committees. This makes some form of law available to every person in the country.

In addition to the president and vice president, Ghana has a number of cabinet ministers. These include the ministers of foreign affairs, defense, communications, finance, food and agriculture, justice, mines and energy, local government and rural development, and trade and industry.

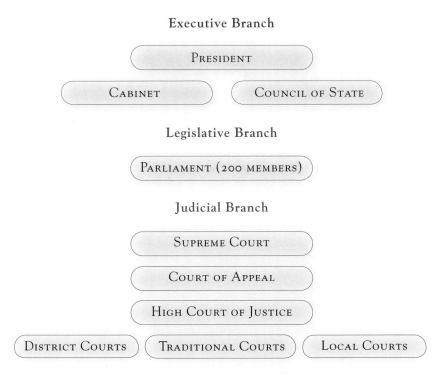

GOVERNMENT OF GHANA

Executive Branch

PRESIDENT

CABINET   COUNCIL OF STATE

Legislative Branch

PARLIAMENT (200 MEMBERS)

Judicial Branch

SUPREME COURT

COURT OF APPEAL

HIGH COURT OF JUSTICE

DISTRICT COURTS   TRADITIONAL COURTS   LOCAL COURTS

A local chief holding court

Role of Chiefs

In practical activities and everyday life, the people are ruled by their chiefs. The lives of people in the rural areas of Ghana are directed by local chiefs. These leaders interpret and apply traditional laws that have a day-to-day impact on the people in their area.

Chiefs are chosen from the senior members of the community—people who are considered descendants of the founders of the community. They usually make their decisions by discussing specific cases with other chiefs until they are able to agree. The position of chief is generally passed down through a family, although not necessarily to the eldest son. Sometimes the brother of the chief is chosen, if he is considered a better choice. The symbol of the chief's position is the stool, and the ceremony in which he becomes the chief is called enstoolment. The chief adds the title *Nana* to his name, meaning "grandfather" or "ancestor." The title refers to the chief's position, not his age.

Accra

Accra is a big city that just grew and grew from its origins as a small town. It has been the capital of Ghana, and before that of the Gold Coast, since 1877. The name *Accra* comes from *nkran*, an Akan word for the black ants found in the area.

National Anthem

"Hail the Name of Ghana"

God bless our homeland Ghana
And make our nation great and strong
Bold to defend for ever
The cause of Freedom and of Right.
Fill our hearts with true humility
Make us cherish fearless honesty
And help us to resist oppressors' rule
With all our will and might for evermore.

Hail to thy name, O Ghana.
To thee we make our solemn vow:
Steadfast to build together
A nation strong in Unity
With our gifts of mind and strength of arm
Whether night or day, in mist or storm
In every need whate'er the call may be
To serve thee, O Ghana, now and evermore.

Raise high the flag of Ghana
And one with Africa advance
Black Star of hope and honor
To all who thirst for liberty
Where the banner of Ghana freely flies
May the way to freedom truly lie
Arise, arise, O sons of Ghanaland
And under God march on for evermore!

The National Flag

Ghana's flag has three horizontal stripes, of red, gold, and green. In the center of the gold section is a black five-pointed star. The green represents the country's forests, the red stands for the blood of those who died fighting for independence, and the gold represents the country's mineral wealth. These are the traditional colors of liberation in Africa. The black star stands for African freedom.

Among the noteworthy buildings are the National Museum, the National Theater, Independence Square, and the new Kwame Nkrumah Mausoleum. In the National Museum, displays such as royal stools, Kente cloth, Asante gold weights, wooden carvings, and drums show the heritage of the country.

In Accra, the poor roads and large number of vehicles have resulted in a practice known as the go-slow traders. Young men and women walk among the cars that are stuck in traffic offering all kinds of goods for sale. Some are very practical, such as food, cooking pots, and clothing. They also offer decorative objects such as framed pictures and large mirrors.

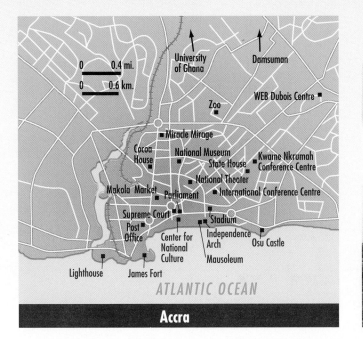

Accra: Did You Know This?

Accra is the largest city in Ghana, with a population of about 1.6 million. The landscape is mostly flat except for some hills such as Legon, where the University of Ghana is located. Accra's economy is based upon its busy port and the manufacture of timber, plywood, clothing, and processed foods. The average summer temperature is 80°F (27°C) and the average winter temperature is 86°F (30°C).

Markets

One of the most important aspects of Ghana's culture is that of the traders. These are men and women who operate small businesses at markets, often outdoors, selling every kind of item imaginable. They sell imported products, locally made goods, and fresh foods. The Makola Market in the center of Accra is the city's main shopping district. The market is a collection of many stalls where people can buy virtually everything they need from food to clothing to household goods.

Bargaining is part of the shopping experience at markets. Prices are not fixed, or printed on signs, and must be agreed to

Outside the Makola Market

after a discussion. Because there is little refrigeration in Ghanaian homes, women shop daily for foods such as meat and fish.

When Jerry Rawlings first seized power in Ghana, he tried to place price controls on food. That put him in a war with the Makola Market women, who wanted to set their own prices. When the market women wouldn't give in, he had the shops bulldozed and then tore down the entire market. The women were back immediately, doing business among the ruins, so finally Rawlings had to give in. He gave up the idea of price controls and had the market rebuilt in 1987, with a new metal roof and a concrete floor.

Jerry Rawlings

Jerry John Rawlings was born on June 22, 1947, to an Ewe mother and a Scottish father. In spite of his mixed heritage, however, he is able to command the loyalty of the Ewe people. He was trained as an officer cadet at Ghana Military Academy and became a flight lieutenant in April 1978. Almost immediately he began a series of actions against the authorities by leading a mutiny of the Ghana armed forces on May 15, 1979. While being detained because of this action, he escaped from custody and led another revolt. That led to a military government headed by Rawlings from June 1979 until September 1979. He stepped aside briefly, from 1979 to 1981, while a civilian government headed by Hilla Limann was in place. Claiming that President Limann's rule was corrupt, he staged another military takeover on December 31, 1981. He headed a military government until 1993, when he was elected president.

In rural areas of Ghana, markets are held only once or twice a week. Rural markets fill in when there are no permanent shops in villages. Here, the people can find all the goods they need, from fabric to food, household appliances, and pottery. Each section of the market specializes in a different product.

A family preparing bread in their home bakery to sell at market

A Land of Resources

A farmer works his small farm plot.

G HANA IS BLESSED WITH NATURAL RESOURCES AND HARD-working people. It is rich in minerals, especially gold. It has land on which to grow enough crops to feed its people and to sell outside the country too.

These benefits must be balanced against the country's economic problems. Ghana's population is growing rapidly, and the country has a huge debt created by the previous government. And, of course, the prices paid for Ghana's main export products, cocoa and gold, are set by world markets.

Opposite: **Workers exiting a gold mine shaft at Obuasi**

Rich stands of forest once covered most of the southwestern part of Ghana, from the border with Ivory Coast all the way east to Accra. Much of this forest has been cleared for farmland. About half the working people have jobs in agriculture, either growing enough food for family use or in the large-scale cocoa (also spelled *cacao*) business.

Large tracts of the best farmland are devoted to production of cocoa beans. Cocoa is grown across the middle section of the country, south of the Black Volta River. Cocoa is a cash crop, which means it is sold outside the country to earn money for the growers. Most of the cocoa is grown on small plots,

Harvesting cocoa pods

measuring less than 7.4 acres (3 ha). Many thousands of Ghanaians are employed on the cocoa farms, where the pods containing the cocoa beans grow on small trees. The Cocoa Marketing Board of Ghana decides how much it will pay the farmers for their cocoa beans. Because there is no competition, the board can set the price very low.

Cocoa Forests

Imagine having fields and fields full of cocoa beans, the basic ingredient for chocolate. But don't think you can just pick a bean and munch on it. It would taste terrible. The cocoa bean is quite bitter before it is processed and turned into chocolate bars. Nearly all of that processing takes place in other countries. Ghana is one of the most important producers of cocoa beans in the world, usually ranking second in production. The major competitors are Brazil, Indonesia, and neighboring Ivory Coast.

When conditions are right, Ghana produces as much as 350,000 metric tons of cocoa beans in one growing season. The older cocoa trees do not produce as many beans as young trees and need to be replaced. The Cocoa Marketing Board plans to sell millions of seedlings to farmers to improve the yield.

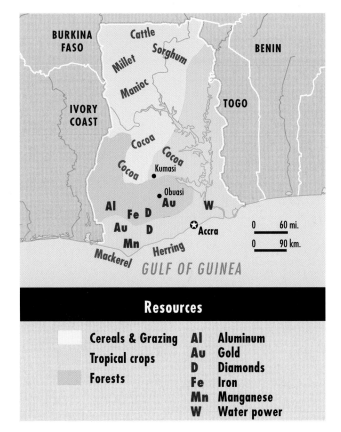

Resources

- Cereals & Grazing
- Tropical crops
- Forests

Al Aluminum
Au Gold
D   Diamonds
Fe Iron
Mn Manganese
W   Water power

Cocoa Growing

The forested region where cocoa beans are grown is the area that receives heavy rainfall, between 40 and 60 inches (102 and 152 cm) each year. Some sections of the Akan lowlands receive as much as 60 to 85 inches (152 to 216 cm). The Pra River Basin is a rich cocoa area, but the South Asante Uplands surrounding Kumasi are the nation's chief producers of cocoa. At a special biological farm, cocoa growers are trying to improve the local variety. They are working with growers from South America, where a different type of cocoa bean is grown.

A basic problem with the way crops were established in Africa is that so much processing has to be done before the products appear on your grocery store shelf. Growing the crop is the most unpredictable part of the process. There is often more money to be made in processing the crop and turning it into a desirable product. That is certainly the case with cocoa beans. In Ghana, the state-owned Cocoa Processing Company produces chocolate almost entirely for the local market.

Cocoa Ups and Downs

The rise and fall of cocoa in Ghana mirrors the country's history over the past 100 years. There are two stories about how cocoa came to Ghana. According to one, it all began in 1878 when a traveler returning to the Gold Coast brought the first cocoa pods into the country. Another legend says that cocoa was first brought into the country by Swiss missionaries, who also tried to grow tea. Either way, under British rule of the Gold Coast colony, planting was carried out on a large scale.

In the 1920s, cocoa became the major support of the entire economy. The Gold Coast's major competitor, Brazil, was struck by a disease that wiped out all of its cocoa trees. During this time, the British company Cadbury controlled the cocoa industry. It was a hard time for the growers. The government fixed the price at which they would buy the cocoa beans from the farmers. All shipping and transportation were arranged by the colonial government. Ghana quickly became a one-crop country, at the mercy of weather and the crops grown in competing countries.

In 1947, the Cocoa Marketing Board was established. It was meant to help the farmers obtain the best new trees, improve transportation, and put the business on a more professional basis. Production grew, and by the end of the 1940s,

In the past, cocoa shipping and transportation were arranged by the British colonial government.

the country was producing half of the world's cocoa. It had a tremendous setback, however, in the late 1940s when a disease called swollen shoot hit the cocoa trees. The government was forced to cut down the affected trees to try to keep the disease from spreading.

Although the cocoa farms recovered and a record crop was achieved in the mid 1960s, the industry fell apart quickly after that. Bad planning, government incompetence, and competition from the Ivory Coast cut into Ghana's share of the market. By 1983, it had just one-eighth of the world market. Production climbed back up in the 1990s, making Ghana one of the biggest producers in the world.

What Ghana Grows, Makes, and Mines

Agriculture (1997)

Roots and tubers	10,500,000 metric tons
Bananas and plantains	1,804,000 metric tons
Cereals	1,770,000 metric tons
Cocoa (cacao)	350,000 metric tons

Manufacturing (1993) *(in Ghanaian cedis)*

Tobacco	71,474,700,000
Footwear	60,350,600,000
Chemical products	40,347,600,000

Mining (1996)

Bauxite	383,370 metric tons
Manganese ore	266,420 metric tons
Gold	50,079 kilograms
Diamonds	773,126 carats

Gold

Ghana, the former Gold Coast, has been associated with gold for more than 500 years. Gold mined in Ghana was being sold and shipped to Europe across the Sahara. In the early days, gold was mined from the streams that run through the gold-rich central belt of Ghana. This process is known as alluvial mining.

Even though mining has been carried out in Ghana for hundreds of years, the country still has plentiful gold reserves. The Obuasi gold mine in the Asante region has been operating since 1907. While it might seem that any gold mine would be profitable, in fact, some mines are more profitable than others. It costs the mine owners money to dig out the gold, and the older and deeper the mine, the more it costs.

A goldsmith in Kumasi making gold jewelry to be worn during ceremonies

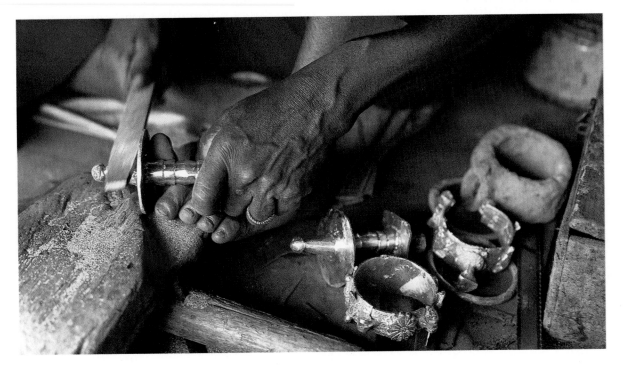

The price of gold is determined by the world market, very much as the price of cocoa is. In the late 1990s, the price of gold hovered around $280–$300 for 1 ounce (28 g). If it cost more than that to produce an ounce of gold, the mine would lose money. The operating cost at Obuasi has been reduced to $230 an ounce.

Obuasi is owned by Ashanti Goldfields, the first African company to be listed on the New York Stock Exchange. A majority share of Ashanti Goldfields is owned by Anglo-American, a South African firm. The mine produces 20 percent of the entire country's income. That's more than just a bonanza for Ashanti Goldfields. It has a very direct effect on Ghana's economy because the government of Ghana owns one-fifth of the mine's stock. Ashanti Goldfields is also a major employer in Ghana, with 10,000 workers.

Ghanaian Currency

The official unit of currency in Ghana is the cedi. Currency is printed in amounts ranging from 10 to 5,000 cedis. It features symbols of the country including its mineral wealth, Kente cloth, and a coat of arms. The cedi is divided into 100 pesewas.

The coat of arms features a shield with the motto "Freedom and Justice." Two eagles support the shield, topped by a black, five-pointed star outlined in gold—the symbol of Ghana as the Black Star of Africa. The colors of the shield are the same as those of the flag—red, gold, and green. A lion in the center of the shield represents the link between Ghana and Britain.

Mining Gold

There are two basic kinds of gold mining and both are used in Ghana. One way is to sink a shaft into the ground, send the miners down to blast out the ore, and then bring it to the surface to be processed. The other way is to work the mine at the surface, as an open-cast mine. The open-cast method is used when the gold is found over a large area and can be mined profitably at the surface. Both methods are used at Obuasi, the largest open-cast gold mine in Africa.

The results of commercial gold mining are very predictable today. The mining engineers know just how much gold is contained in each ton of earth. They know that if a certain number of tons of earth are scooped up and processed each day, a certain number of ounces of gold will be produced. That is what is meant by *proven gold reserves*. Underground gold mining has been practiced in Ghana since the 1860s. This kind of large-scale mining requires a huge investment in equipment, and in Ghana it quickly led to financial control of the mines by outsiders—Europeans. The British controlled the gold mining industry during the colonial period.

The rich Asante gold mines are located in the Axim-Kononga belt. A mining area may stretch for miles, so mining engineers decide which part of the area to develop first. In addition to Ashanti Goldfields, a number of other companies operate in Ghana, including Obosso Goldfields, Ghana Gold Mines, Bonte Gold, State Gold Mining Corporation, and Dunkwa Goldfields.

Timber

The great stretches of forested land in Ghana have been harvested for timber for 100 years. In some areas of the country, sawmills were built so that the logs could be processed into timber before they were shipped out to markets around the world. Timber was so important to the economy during the colonial period that rail lines were built to the forest areas to bring out the logs.

Fishing

The waters off the Ghanaian coast offer rich fishing. The number of fish taken from the waters by Ghanaian commercial fishermen has increased steadily since 1970, reaching more than 300,000 tons. The catch has gone down recently, however, because foreign fishing boats, mostly from Japan, have taken huge amounts of fish. A large commercial tuna-processing plant in Tema is owned by StarKist Seafood.

After the fish are caught, many are preserved by salting, drying, and smoking, then traded inland. Communal smoking ovens are used. When there are not enough fish available in the local waters, the Fante of Ghana sometimes travel along the coast, ranging as far as Senegal to the northwest and Cameroon to the southeast. They follow the currents where the fish may be found.

Working together to prepare fishing nets

Women on the Atlantic coast buying fish from the day's catch

Women sometimes work along the shore, especially in fish processing and marketing, but only men are permitted in the fishing canoes along the coast. Freshwater fishing in Lake Volta also yields many tons of fish. Men go out in handmade dugout canoes along the lake's long shoreline and fish to feed their families.

Ports and Harbors

Ghana's long coastline does not provide natural harbors for large ships. Two artificial harbors were built, one at Takoradi and one at Tema. These ports allow ships to load up crops grown in Ghana and unload goods from elsewhere. There are a number of inland harbors along the Lake Volta shoreline.

Hard Times in Ghana

Rule by Jerry Rawlings has been marked by a tightening of control over the press. Rawlings shut down an independent radio station and seized its equipment. In 1998, two newspaper editors were jailed for a month for criticizing his wife.

In 1995, a new 17.5 percent tax, called VAT (value-added tax), was imposed on goods and services, but it led to such widespread demonstrations that it was withdrawn. In 1998, the Rawlings government tried again to apply this tax. This time they held education sessions for the people who sell goods. If the tax is applied, it will be a big burden on the poorest people—those who can barely afford the goods anyway.

Where Is the Power?

In 1998, the growth of Ghana's economy was severely threatened by a shortage of electricity. The major source of energy is powered by the water that fills up Lake Volta and spills over Akosombo Dam. The water in Lake Volta accumulates between July and November. It is up to the authorities to determine how much water can be allowed to spill over the dam.

When the rains are less than normal and there isn't enough water spilling over the dam to generate power, Ghana suffers from a lack of electricity. In 1998, for the second time in ten years, drought created a serious shortage of electric power. Traffic lights and streetlights didn't work, small businesses had to cut back on their workforce, and goods that depend on power-driven machinery couldn't be produced.

Ashanti Goldfields, one of the nation's most important industries, is building its own power plant. It will use gas rather than hydroelectric power. Other plans are in the works to create new sources of energy. A new power plant that operates on diesel fuel has been built at Takoradi by General Electric Corporation. This plant supplies electricity without disruption because it does not depend on rainfall. Small power stations are also being built around the country to lighten the burden on Akosombo. Ghana is also looking into solar power, taking advantage of the tremendous amount of sunshine the country enjoys.

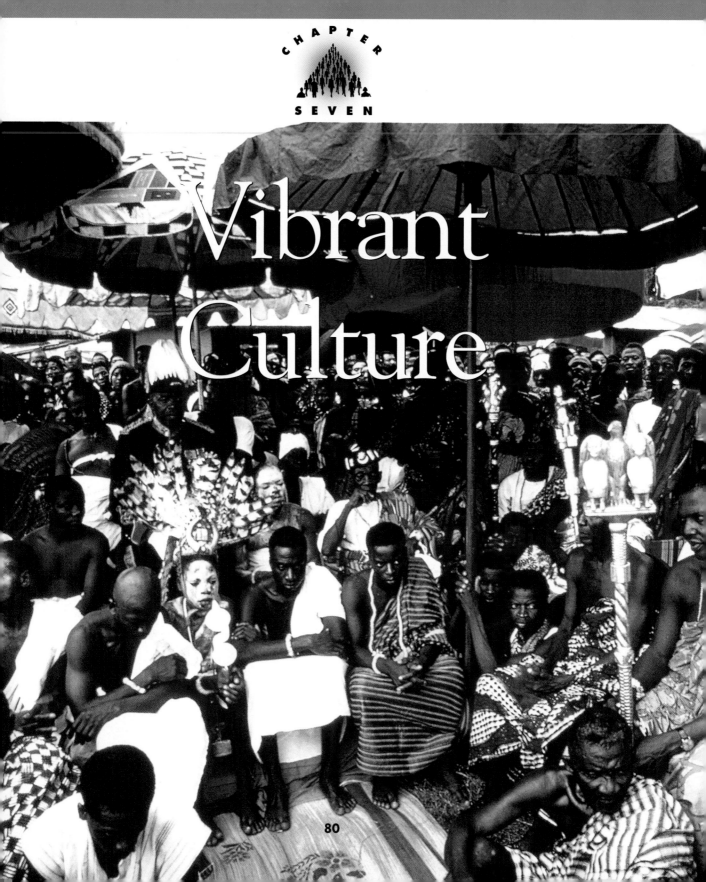

CHAPTER SEVEN

Vibrant Culture

80

THE PEOPLE OF GHANA HAVE SOME OF THE RICHEST CULTURES in all of Africa. Their cultures dictate the clothes they wear, the foods they eat, and the way they live surrounded by extended families. Culture is expressed especially in the brilliant cloths made in Ghana and in the gold objects that are part of the ceremonies of the Asante people. Each ethnic group—the Asante, the Fante, the Ewe, the Ga, and the rest—has its distinct customs and material objects.

Opposite: **A gathering of chiefs at the Nmayem festival**

The baskets these men are weaving will be sold at the National Culture Market.

Asante girls fetching water
from a stream near Kumasi

The total population of Ghana is about 18.5 million people. It is a very young population, with children under fifteen making up 45 percent of the total. Only 3 percent of the people are older than sixty-five. About one-third live in urban areas. The Akan, which includes the Asante and the Fante, are the largest group. They live in the south-central part of the country. The Mossi-Dagomba live in the north, near the border with Burkina Faso; the Ewe live in the east, next to Togo; and the Ga people live in the coastal region. Each group takes great pride in its language, its culture, its festivals, and its ceremonies.

Language

When the European powers divided up Africa among themselves, they insisted on the use of their own European languages. They did not think it necessary to learn the language of the people they ruled. As a result, Ghana came to be an English-speaking country surrounded by three French-speaking countries—Ivory Coast, Burkina Faso, and Togo. Anyone from the Gold Coast who wanted to play a role in the development of his or her own country had to learn to speak English.

Who Lives in Ghana?

Black African	99.8%
Major Groups	
Akan	44%
Mossi-Dagomba	16%
Ewe	13%
Ga	8%
European and other	0.2%

The people who came in contact with the British learned English. They were able to trade with the English and learn their ways of living. More important, this common language helped to tie all the people of the region together. Those in the more remote northern part of the country did not have this contact and remain more isolated to this day.

Seventy-two distinct languages are spoken within the borders of Ghana. These languages break down into two major language groups—Kwa, spoken by the Akan and Ewe who live south of the Volta River, and Gur, spoken by those living north of the Volta.

Population of Ghana's Largest Cities (est.)

Accra	1,600,000
Kumasi	1,000,000
Sekondi-Takoradi	300,000
Tema	250,000

These villagers, who are carrying harvested tomatoes, speak a dialect of the Kwa language group.

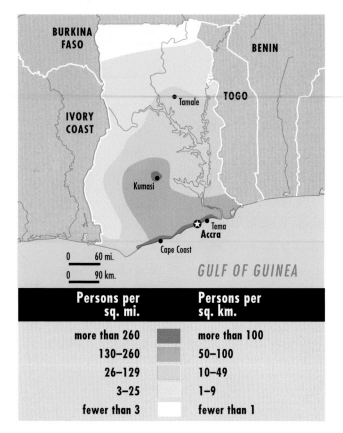

Persons per sq. mi.		Persons per sq. km.
more than 260		more than 100
130–260		50–100
26–129		10–49
3–25		1–9
fewer than 3		fewer than 1

Population distribution in Ghana

How would a new nation choose one of these languages without discriminating against the others? The growing use of English gave the Ghanaians a common language and enabled them to talk to one another. It helped to pave the way for the independent country of Ghana and helped make nationalism possible. So English is the official language of Ghana, but African languages are widely spoken.

Many Ghanaians speak several languages. Often, these languages are related to one another, such as Akan, Asante, and Fante. People who spend a lot of time in Accra often learn to speak Ga, the local language. Ewe, in the Volta region, is a more difficult language and harder to learn.

Naming Children

People who speak an Akan language often name their children according to the day of the week on which they are born. When you meet such a person, you always know his or her birth day. There are different names for boys and girls. In the Fante language, starting with Sunday, boys are named Kwesi, Kwadwo, Kwabena, Kweku, Yaw, Kofi, and Kwame. So we know that UN Secretary-General Kofi Annan was born on Friday, and Ghana's first president, Kwame Nkrumah, was born on Saturday. Names for girls, starting on Sunday, are Esi, Adwoa, Abena, Akua, Yaa, Afua, and Amma.

Kente Cloth

Asante culture is expressed in many ways. It can be seen in the gold objects made for members of the royal family, and in the vibrant fabric known as Kente cloth. The brilliant patterns of Kente cloth have become popular in the United States, especially among African-Americans.

When it was first made in the seventeenth century, Kente cloth could be worn only by Asante royalty. The threads for the cloths made for the royal family often came from imported silk. Not only was the cloth restricted to royalty, but each pattern was woven for a particular king.

An Asante man proudly wears Kente cloth.

The name *Kente* is derived from *kenten*, which means "a basket." The patterns originally were woven from raffia fibers, and the cloth looked like a basket. The weavers call the cloth by its Asante name, *nsaduaso*, which means "a cloth hand-woven on a loom." Kente cloth had its origins in the Ghanaian village of Bonwire.

Strip Weaving

Kente is woven on looms that are 4 inches (10 cm) wide. The narrow strips are sewn together to make fabric. Garments are then fashioned from the fabric. Often, the fabric is worn as a simple toga, draped over one shoulder. Each pattern is named, usually in reference to events that took place during the reign of an Asante king. These specific patterns represent such

Kente cloth is woven in narrow strips.

qualities as strength, bravery, beauty, valor, and leadership. Brilliant colors—especially yellow, orange, blue, and red—are mixed in intricate patterns. When the strips are sewn together, they merge into a flowing pattern. A weaver who creates a new pattern is recognized as someone of great talent.

Some patterns that commemorate important events now represent the history and values of the people. The cloth communicates shared beliefs and values such as military might, courage, leadership, beauty, creativity, and bravery. Instead of painting a portrait of a brave military leader or a heroic king, the weaver created a cloth that demonstrated those qualities. The high cost of Kente cloth puts it out of reach of many people who would like to wear these distinctive patterns.

Weaving Meanings

Among the important patterns are *Emaa da*, which means "it has not happened before." The Asante king who first saw the pattern was struck by its originality and gave it that name. *Kyeretwie*, which means "lion catcher," was designed to commemorate the skills of warriors. The cloth named *Akyempem*, meaning "thousands of shields," celebrates the unity of the military men and women who defended the kingdom. Because the cloth takes so much time to produce, a large piece of Kente fabric indicates not only a person of royal status but also someone of wealth.

The Ewe people of eastern Ghana weave their own variety of Kente cloth. The Ewe cloth is distinguished by its tweedy look, created when different-colored threads are twined to form the warp threads on the loom. The complicated weaving process requires great technical and artistic skill on the part of the weaver.

Adinkra Cloth

Another fabric that speaks through its patterns is Adinkra cloth, also from the Asante culture. The word *Adinkra* means "farewell" and originally was associated with funerals and other rites of passage. According to the widely accepted myth of origin, Adinkera, or Adinkra, a king of the region known as Ivory Coast, tried to copy the Asante's revered Golden Stool. In the war that resulted, Adinkera was slain. The cloth he wore when he was killed featured the stamping technique used to create Adinkra cloth.

While the whole pattern of a Kente cloth is created to communicate a message, Adinkra cloth is built upon a vocabulary of symbols. More than eighty symbols are used as design elements on goods made by the Asante. Adinkra symbols represent the thinking, the history, and the beliefs of the Asante people.

The process begins with a solid-color cloth. Designs are carved into a stamping die made from a calabash—a hard-skinned gourd that grows on a vine. Then natural dyes are made from the bark of the badia tree. The designer first draws squares on the fabric, forming rows. Then the symbols are stamped repeatedly in these squares. Because so many

The patterns on Adinkra cloth are stamped onto the fabric.

different symbols are used, the cloth is very lively looking.

The vocabulary of Adinkra symbols is based on Asante proverbs that describe the events of everyday life. They are sometimes patterned after forms found in nature as well as those created by the people. The graphic shapes have been in use for more than 100 years.

Symbolic Meaning

Some of the Adinkra symbols begin with simple, universally recognized shapes such as *Akoma*, the heart. When used as an Adinkra symbol, in addition to its usual symbolic meaning of love, Akoma also means patience, faithfulness, and endurance. But when the heart is drawn so that the lines are extended into curlicues both inside and out, it has completely different meanings. One is *Sankofa*, which means "go back to fetch it." This means you can learn from the wisdom of the past. By retrieving the past, you can build on it to create a better future.

A Culture of Gold

Gold is a vital part of the Asante culture. Gold was taken from streams where panning techniques separated the gold from the sediment. Women traditionally panned the gold, while men dug the pits from which the gold-bearing ore was taken. Having so much gold available inspired the development of fine goldsmithing techniques. During the fourteenth and fifteenth centuries, the Portuguese were deeply involved in trading for gold from the Akan region. Much of this gold was acquired from Mande traders.

Working with Gold

Gold is a soft metal that can be worked with simple tools. Gold objects can be molded by a method known as lost-wax casting, or beaten into very thin sheets, or drawn into extremely fine wire. Patterns can be raised from below the surface or engraved on the surface. This extraordinary flexibility, along with its availability, was the basis of its lavish use by the royal members of the Asante culture. Gold was the basic element of trade in the region from the sixteenth century and was traded for popular European products. Chief among these were the glass beads made in Venice, Italy, that became known as trading beads These beautiful beads known as *millefiori* ("a thousand flowers") were so highly desired that they came to be traded for human beings—slaves.

Bead Village

In the village of Odumase-Krobo, the Dipo-Krobo festival takes place. This ritual marks the coming of age of Dipo girls, and everything about it involves strands of glass beads made by hand in the village. Powdered glass is placed in a mold with five little cups, colors are added, and then the beads are fired

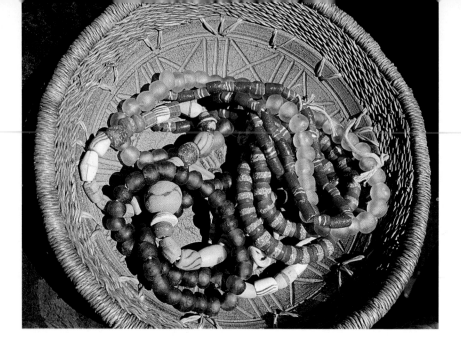

Glass beads are made by hand in the village of Odumase-Krobo

in a kiln. These beads are strung together into long ropes. During the ceremony, which takes place over several days, the girls wear different-colored beads. This is a very old tradition among the Krobo people.

The Dipo-Krobo festival usually takes place in April, but the exact date varies. It can be delayed because the moon is not in the right phase, for example. Or it may be delayed because the chief hasn't gathered enough money to pay for all the food needed for the many people who come to take part in the ceremony.

In the past, a girl would be married after the ceremony. Now she is more likely to be in school, and so she must travel home for the ceremony. The beads she wears belong to her family, and she shows them off proudly during the ceremony. A woman acquires beads throughout her life. She inherits some beads from her mother, she buys some herself, and her husband may give her strands of beads.

Asantehene

The center of the Asante kingdom, and its world of gold, is Kumasi. There, the Asantehene, the king of the Asante people, holds traditional power over his people. His status is shown in the gold that surrounds him at ceremonial occasions. Unlike the fictional King Midas, the Asantehene enjoys his life as well as his gold. Former Asantehene Otumfuo Opuku Ware II (right) wore masses of gold jewelry, so much that his arms and ankles were too heavy to lift.

Otumfuo Osei Tutu II became Asantehene in April 1999. Like the king before him, who studied law and held several government positions, the new Asantehene is well educated. He studied accounting in London. When he became Asantehene he left behind his old name, Barima Nana Kwaku Dua.

Rites of Passage

Coming-of-age ceremonies, those moments that mark the transition from one stage of life to the next, are celebrated by the whole community. Each stage is honored and ties the individual to the ongoing history of the people. From the moment of birth, a Ghanaian is a member of a specific community.

Ga babies are named in a public ceremony called an *outdooring*. Ceremonies are also held when a boy or girl reaches puberty. This marks the time when the child begins to take on the responsibilities of an adult. All the way through life to death itself, the Ghanaians combine the rituals of traditional African religion with the religions that were imported to their land. They feel comfortable following both paths, taking comfort and support from each.

Customs

The different ethnic groups of Ghana are divided into two types of society. In some, including the Ga, children trace their ancestry through their fathers. In others, including the Akan, they trace their ancestry through their mothers. This is an important difference because it determines how a child inherits property.

Marriage

Traditional marriage ceremonies, known as "customary" marriages, are at the heart of Ghanaian culture. Even people who get married in a church and have a Western-style wedding often have a customary marriage ceremony first. Family members play a major role in these ceremonies.

The several stages in the marriage ceremony involve the payment of different kinds of fees. In the first stage, this is simply a round of drinks for the bride's father. At the engagement ceremony, the bride's parents are given valuable gifts, including domestic animals such as cows and sheep. The engagement ceremony really marks the beginning of the couple's marriage. More presents are given to finalize the marriage. The marriage is a contract between the extended families and creates obligations, duties, and rights that will continue throughout their lives. The two families are tied together by this marriage.

Children

The greatest blessing for a marriage is children. A marriage without children is seen as a curse and usually ends in a separation

or divorce. When a child arrives, it is a time of great joy and ceremony. The baby is kept inside for the first week. On the eighth day, at the home of the father's family, the baby is brought out to see daylight and to be seen for the first time. The Ga celebrate with an outdooring. The Akan have a brief ceremony after the birth and then wait longer to name the baby. They do this because of the fear that the baby might not survive. If a child died after being given the name of an ancestor, it would be a tragedy. In the past, many babies died as a result of inadequate medical care both before and after the birth.

Children bring great joy to a family. This woman has wrapped her toddler to carry him on her back.

The practice of polygamy—having more than one wife at once—is a part of some people's lives, especially in the rural areas where farmwork is shared. Although the Muslim religion allows a man to have as many as four wives if he can afford to support them, the Christian religion says a man should have only one wife at at time. But in Ghana, even some Christians have more than one wife. It is a sign of prestige to have a large family, and having more than one wife assures that a man will have many children. This is in keeping with the code that covers moral and social behavior.

Children learn by example from family members—including aunts and uncles, cousins and grandparents—and learn to show respect to all of them. This extended family gives children a strong feeling of belonging to a community.

The Akan people, a group that includes the Asante, have many proverbs. These are often comments on proper behavior. The importance of living a good life, of doing the right thing, is summed up in the proverb "Disgrace is worse than death." Honoring your relatives is clear from the proverb "If your elders take care of you while you are cutting your teeth, you must in turn take care of them while they are losing theirs." Some offer practical advice: "If you are in hiding, don't light a fire." And some are very wise: "There is no medicine to cure hatred" and "No one tests the depth of a river with both feet."

In Ghana, showing hospitality is considered part of having a good character—the basis of being a good person. Sharing is also basic to good character. People in Ghana have a duty to take care of their relatives. If relatives show up at your house, you must allow them to stay and you must feed them. Although this is sometimes a great burden, people still feel obliged to share whatever they have.

Painting Houses

In the northern countryside, women not only take care of the household, but they also build a certain type of house. The walls are made of a mixture of mud and dung, often combined with a binding material such as straw or pieces of plants. The material can be shaped and molded to any form the maker desires. Dried mud, which we call adobe, creates a cool place in which to live, a big advantage in a tropical climate. Although the mud needs frequent repairs, it is readily available—and it costs nothing.

In the region of Navrongo-Saboro, women decorate their mud houses in beautiful geometric patterns. They make their own paints using materials found in nature. Each woman creates her own design and draws it right on the wall, using grasses as a brush or applying the color directly with her fingers. The patterns are taken from traditional designs but they are combined

Geometric patterns and large pottery urns decorate this house.

in original ways. Some women draw patterns directly into the mud before it dries, turning the entire house into a sculpture. Some patterns imitate the rows of kernels on an ear of corn.

Houses in other regions may have mud walls and tin roofs. Many people have houses made of cement blocks, more suitable to rainy areas, and these also have tin roofs. In the cities, most people live in houses with a small yard where they can keep a few chickens or a pig. Even close to the heart of Accra, chickens cluck and pigs oink. In very wealthy sections, people live in large modern houses that we would call mansions.

Education

Ghana devotes 40 percent of the national budget to education. In 1974, primary schools and middle schools were made free—and compulsory—for all children. However, parents must pay for books, supplies, and school uniforms, which are required.

Even though the law requires that children attend school for at least eight years, not every child is able to go to school. In areas of remote villages, where few people live, schools are far apart and the closest one may be too far away.

These rural children are being taught in their own language. English is the primary language for instruction of older students.

Instruction in this Cape Coast classroom is in English.

In primary school, children are usually taught in their first language for the first three years. Then English is introduced, and it becomes the language of instruction. The British system of standardized tests has been introduced. Students must pass these tests before they can move on to the next grade. Only a small percentage of students continues past the tenth grade.

At every level, the percentage of boys attending school is higher than that of girls. Girls, especially in rural areas, are expected to be homemakers, while boys are expected to support families and therefore need more education. About 40 percent of adults in Ghana can read. There is a great shortage of books, however, because they are expensive to import.

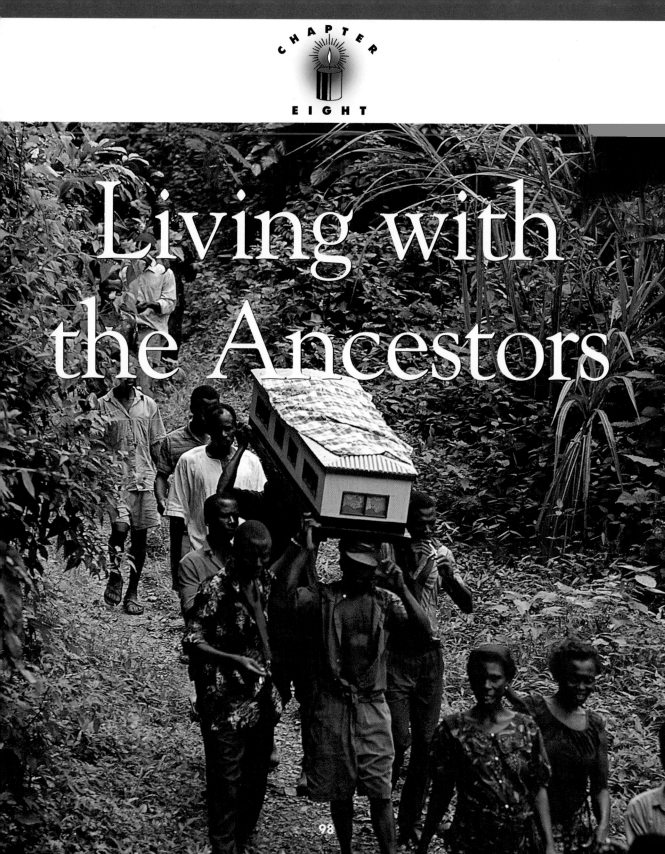

Living with the Ancestors

Traditional Religions

Before Europeans and Arabs arrived in the region that is now Ghana, the people followed their own traditional religions. These religions are based on a strong belief that life is a continuous line, and that one's parents and grandparents—and all those who came before—have a strong influence on the lives of people living today. Traditional religion believes in a supreme figure, or god, known as *Nyame* in the Akan language and *Mawu* in the Ewe language.

People don't worship this supreme god directly because it is too remote. Instead, they communicate through lesser gods who are felt to be a part of the entire natural world. That world—rivers and trees and mountains—was created by the supreme god.

Different ethnic groups put more importance on different parts of the natural world. The Asante, for example, see their lesser or minor god in the Tano River. Each local area has a local god. Individuals also worship a personal god, one who relates to that person's clan, community, or household. The Krobo people call their minor gods *dzemawoi*, which means "guardians of the worlds." The Akan call their minor gods *abosom*, which is related to their word for stones.

The spirit world is very real in these religions—as real as the people in one's own family and community. This connection is expressed in the way daily responsibilities are carried out. For example, it is believed that a person who lives a good

Opposite: **Members of a funeral procession carrying a house-shaped coffin**

life can improve the well-being of those who have already died. Everyone is linked to the spiritual world through their deceased ancestors. They are a presence in everyday life, and people believe that their ancestors are watching them all the time.

Sometimes an ancestor will come back to life in order to complete a task that was left undone. The ancestor does this in the form of one's children. For this reason, it is important to have children, to be sure the family line continues. It is very sad when a couple is unable to have children because then the ancestors have no way to return to life.

Ancestors and family are very important in traditional religions of Ghana. People are linked to the spirit world through their ancestors.

Role of Priests

Priests help people to maintain this connection among life, the world of the dead, and the gods. They are also important in healing because many people believe some illnesses have spiritual causes and therefore can be cured by a spiritual person. It is not unusual for an educated Ghanaian to consult such a person, known as an oracle or a medium.

Christianity

Christian missionaries have been active in Ghana since the Portuguese arrived in the fifteenth century. The Christian church became a strong presence in Ghana during the nineteenth century when the Presbyterian and Methodist missionaries arrived. As in other parts of Africa, they established schools to attract people they wished to convert to their religion.

A Palm Sunday procession

The Africans had a great thirst for education, but the colonial rulers rarely offered them a chance to go to school. The missions held out this gift of education, but it came with a price. The student had to accept the religion of the mission. Even today, most major

A Christian Methodist secondary school

Religions of Ghana

Christian	43%
Traditional	38%
Muslim	12%
Other (Hindu, Buddhist, Jewish, Baha'i)	7%

Sunday worshipers dancing in church

secondary schools in Ghana are church or mission schools. However, any student can attend a church school today without being a member of that particular religion.

In general, most people in the southern part of the country are Christians, while those in the north tend to be Muslims. Many people follow traditional religions. The many branches of Christianity in Ghana include Methodist, Anglican, Mennonite, Presbyterian, Evangelical Presbyterian, and Baptist churches.

Many Ghanaians who practice Christianity or who identify themselves as Christians also keep their traditional beliefs. They combine the two religious belief systems and fix the mixture to suit their needs.

Islamic Schools

Arrival of the imam, a religious leader, at the central mosque in Kumasi

Muslim men in northern Ghana studying the Koran

While Christianity was brought by missionaries, who arrived for that purpose, Islam traveled to Ghana along the trade routes. In the Muslim areas, as in the Christian areas, schools began as religious institutions. However, Islamic schools offer a more limited kind of education focusing almost entirely on religious instruction. This centers around the study of the Koran, the Muslim holy book. There is little room for more advanced studies or for scientific learning. This has limited the lives of the Muslims so that they tend to live on a lower economic level than the Christians.

Traditional ways of living and thinking still have a strong grip on the people. When someone moves to the city, that person keeps close ties to the other family members. In African societies, the extended family includes aunts, uncles, and cousins—everyone to whom a person is related by blood. If one member of the family is sent away to university, that person will later be responsible for the financial well-being of his entire extended family.

Funerals

The connection with one's ancestors is crucial in the life of Ghanaians. Honoring the dead is a year-long expression but it is not an expression of grief. People honor the deceased by talking about the life the person lived. The friends and family celebrate the life by taking part in the preparations for the funeral.

When a person dies, it is a sign of respect for many people to help prepare the body for burial. The person must be bathed and prepared for the next stage, which is seen as a continuation of the life lived on earth. A person's favorite possessions are buried with the body for use in the next life. The spirits of the next life must be happy with the

Women take turns beating fufu, a dish that will be served to funeral guests.

materials that are being offered. People who come to pay their respects often hold conversations with the dead, talking about experiences they had together and wondering about how the person will be taken care of in the future. As many as 2,000 people may attend a funeral.

A special Adinkra cloth is often made for the occasion. The women wear the cloth, printed with symbols and a saying, wrapping it around them to form skirts and turbans, and sewing it into blouses. This shows respect for the deceased. The cloth is often red, a color associated with sad occasions such as the death of a relative. Red is also used in times of war or national crisis.

Fantasy Coffins

In Teshi, a small town near Accra, a special kind of business has been created. In the past, a special coffin in the shape of an eagle was made for a chief, by carver Ata Owoo. That inspired Kane Kwei to make a special coffin for a relative of his in 1956. The business soon took off and became a small industry. Kwei's cousin Paa Joe continues the work, making ten coffins a year. These fantasy coffins are made in shapes that reflect the life or interests of the deceased person. A taxi driver who drove an old Mercedes-Benz was buried in a smaller version of his car. Another person's life was celebrated by a coffin shaped like his fishing boat, complete with eight paddlers.

It takes up to 300 pieces of wood to make a fantasy coffin. Some people order them well in advance of the time they expect to need them because it takes as long as a month to carve such a coffin. However, if a person dies unexpectedly, or if the coffin is not ready in time, that is not a problem. It is common for a funeral to take place some weeks—or even months—after the person's death.

Rhythms
of Life

L IFE IN GHANA IS A RICH MIX OF CULTURES AND TRADITIONS. Although more and more people are moving to the cities, they never forget their own cultures. They are expressed in every-day things such as the market, the foods, the music, and the festivals. It's in the way women dress in traditional fabrics. It's in the way people greet one another. They speak softly, they smile with genuine warmth, and they share their traditions with great joy. The long tradition of culture, unbroken over the centuries, has made Ghanaians very secure in knowing exactly who they are and where they come from.

Opposite: **Drums are an important part of festivals and funerals.**

Kofi Annan

The Ghanaian who is best known around the world today is Kofi Annan. This soft-spoken man is secretary-general of the United Nations (UN), an extraordinarily difficult job. All the problems of the world, all the wars, all the refugees, are supposed to be solved by the UN, and everyone looks to the UN's secretary-general as the chief problem solver.

Kofi Annan is the son of a Fante chief and was born on April 8, 1938. He grew up near Kumasi, but most of his adult life has been spent outside Ghana. He attended Macalaster College in Minnesota, where he received an undergraduate degree in economics. He went back to school at the age of thirty-three, earning a master's degree from the Massachusetts Institute of Technology. Except for a brief period as managing director of the Ghana Tourist Development Company,

his entire career has been at the United Nations. Annan is the first secretary-general to reach that position from the inside—he worked at various UN agencies including the World Health Organization and the High Commission on Refugees. He speaks several African languages as well as English and French, two of the official UN languages.

Women at a Ga harvest festival

Rhythms of Ghana

Ghana without music is a book without words. You can't understand the story if you don't hear the music. In fact, Ghanaians even use drums to communicate. These are called "talking drums." They make sounds that imitate the Asante language and allow people to send important messages and news from one village to another. But drums are much more than a way of speaking. They also provide the vital music that enables dancers to communicate too.

Both men and women dance. Their dancing has traditional movements that immediately identify the dancers as Ghanaian. They have a way of moving different parts of their bodies to different beats, all at the same time, in very complicated rhythms. Drums are made from wood and from gourds. Drums are a vital part of festivals and funerals, where they may be played for hours.

Among the Asante, the Asantehene may show his authority by performing a special dance. He might even be judged according to his dancing skill. Dances tell stories. In one dance, a man who is hungry disguises himself as a woman so that he may enter a market and steal a chicken. Through his dancing, he imitates the way women walk. Sometimes a dance tells a piece of history. The Ewe created a dance to show how they migrated into the community where they now live. In this dance, the dancers imitate the movements of a bird with their arms. They show how the Ewe followed a bird on their migration from neighboring Benin to the land in the west—Ghana.

Ewe men and women dancing

Modern music, called "highlife," began to develop in Ghana and then spread farther into West Africa. It is a vibrant style of music that combines European ballroom dance techniques with traditional African dance. Highlife has crossed boundaries all through central Africa and into the south as well. When U.S. president Bill Clinton visited Ghana in March 1998, highlife music provided the entertainment and several bands performed for the presidential party.

Traditional Healers

Although modern medicine is practiced in Ghana, some people turn to traditional healers. These healers have a wide knowledge of herbal remedies and are skillful in treating diseases. They also offer an alternative to the official health-care system, which is unable to reach many people who need it. In addition, many cannot afford Western-style medicine. Healers make herbs, weeds, and tree bark into potions, which they apply during ceremonies that include a mix of African songs and dances as well as Christian prayers. The healers treat people with mental as well as physical ailments. Recently, the Ghanaian Health Ministry has reached out to the traditional healers in an effort to stop the spread of AIDS.

Festivals

Most festivals in Ghana are celebrated by specific groups of people. Many of them celebrate the harvest of the crop, the center of daily life. The best known of these is the *Yam* festival, celebrated by the Akan people. There is also a fish festival called *Bakatue*. At the beginning of a festival, people traditionally cleared the paths leading to their villages. In fact, there is a specific festival known as *Akwambo*, which is the path-clearing festival.

People who live in the cities often travel back to the home villages to celebrate traditional festivals. The *Homowo*,

Runners at the *Homowo* festival in Teshi

a harvest festival, is celebrated by the Ga. It is held in August and September in Teshi to give thanks for a successful harvest. This is a particularly colorful festival. Runners celebrate this annual event by racing around and around the village. They form teams and are often sponsored by local companies, which provide their tracksuits. Children take part as well, joining in the running. There is no finish line, it's just a continuous race to show their happiness for a successful harvest. In a country where so many people depend on the food they produce, this is a major celebration.

The *Hogbetsotso* festival is celebrated by the Ewe people in the Volta region. It marks a time in history when the Ewe people escaped from a terrible ruler. One of the best-known

Ama Ata Aidoo

Ama Ata Aidoo has been writing about her culture and her country her whole life. Her first play, *The Dilemma of a Ghost*, was published in 1964 when she was at the University of Ghana. Aidoo came of age when Ghana was still a British colony. She was born in 1940, the daughter of a chief. Her plays reflect the struggles of the country, especially after independence. She was greatly disappointed when Ghana's independence turned out so badly. Her writings also reflect the difficult role of women in African society. One of the themes of her writing is that of the brain drain from Ghana. Many of the best-trained and best-educated people left the country to find political freedom as well as economic opportunity—two important ingredients that were missing in Ghana for so many years. She wants Ghanaians to rely on themselves. Although Ghanaians thought independence would cure all their problems, she wrote, "There is no use screaming about how independent you are by driving away the colonialists if you do not make independence meaningful." Now that a measure of political freedom has returned, she also writes about a well-known figure, the *been-to*. This is the educated person who has been to a foreign country and is now back in Ghana, full of new knowledge. This person is a bridge between the two cultures but often finds he or she no longer feels at home in either culture. Her books include *Our Sister Killjoy* and *No Sweetness Here*.

festivals in Ghana is the *Aboakyir*, celebrated on the first Saturday in May. It is a celebration of the hunt, and the goal is to capture a live antelope.

Literature

Ghana has many writers who use their own cultures and experiences as the basis for their books. Kwame Anthony Appiah is well known for his work, including the book *In My Father's House*. He now teaches at Harvard University. Kofi Awoonor is a poet and novelist. Although he writes in English, he uses his Ewe culture to talk about life in Ghana since independence. His first novel was *This Earth, My Brother: An Allegorical Tale of Africa*, the story of a young lawyer trying to understand his newly independent society.

This barbershop sign shows men's hairstyles.

Hairstyles

Hairstyles are important in Ghana for both men and women. Beautifully painted signs in the markets show the variety of hairstyles each hairdresser offers. These signs have become collector's items. West Africa is known for the intricate, braided hairdos the women wear. These braided styles influenced African-Americans who adopted the braided look because it is so well suited to their hair.

A village soccer game

 Sports

In most African countries, the national sport is soccer. Boys, both small and large, play soccer wherever they can find a piece of ground. Ghana's national team, the Black Stars, is avidly supported. It takes part in the World Cup as well as the African Nations Cup, the second most important soccer event. In 1998, Ghana qualified as one of the Group One teams in the African Nations Cup. Over a period of nine months, teams travel all over Africa to compete. Ghana's six matches were played against the national teams from Cameroon, Mozambique, and Eritrea. The matches were held from October 1998 through June 1999.

Kim Tyrone-Grant of Ghana in the 1997 World Cup qualifier

A Famous Boxer

Ghana is also known for producing successful boxers. Some of the best boxers in their divisions were born in Ghana. They usually compete in the lighter-weight divisions known as featherweight. One of the most enduring Ghanaian boxers is Accra's Azumah Nelson, a three-time world champion in his weight class.

Nelson has fought in matches all over the world and has been compared to the best athletes in any sport. He is very popular in Ghana and his fights are followed closely. He was the first African named to the International Boxing Hall of Fame. In November 1998, he announced his retirement after nineteen years in the ring.

Tradition and Change

I N GHANA, THE HOT CLIMATE PLAYS A LARGE ROLE IN DECIDING how people live their lives. Long before sunrise, people are already up and about, starting their daily work. They try to get as much done as possible before the heat of the day has built

This woman works on a palm oil plantation.

up. The farmers go off to their farms, often walking several miles to get to their land. They do the hard work in the cooler morning hours and try to finish for the day before noon. Each family has its own land to farm. Some of the farms are quite large, and the people call them plantations. They grow food for the family and also food to sell. To sell the food, though, they must live close to a road where there is some kind of transportation. This is still a problem in Ghana.

Women work even harder than men because they work all day long. Most women in the villages farm land for their own families. Women also have to collect firewood for their cooking fire. As they use up all the wood around their homes, they must walk farther and farther. They also have to walk to get water and carry it back home, balanced on their heads. Some villages have tanks to collect rainwater for home use and for farms. Some villages have a pump that the women use to bring up water. Even when the pump is far from home, the women must carry the water all the way back. Children often work very hard too, carrying water and firewood.

Cooking takes up a great deal of time because everything is made by hand. Most villagers do not have canned food or even prepared flour. The foods must be prepared every day. And while a woman is working, she usually has her youngest child on her back, securely wrapped up in a cloth.

In the north, the cattle must be taken to a field where they can graze on the tall grasses, and they must also be watered. All of this involves a lot of walking back and forth in the hot sun.

A village market

In the bustling markets of Accra and Kumasi, the unique spirit of Ghana is everywhere. Women in traditional clothes fill the crowded marketplace, shopping for food and household goods, as they have for generations.

The friendliness of the Ghanaian people and the continuing hope for Ghana's future swept over U.S. president Bill Clinton when he made Ghana the first stop on his six-nation tour of Africa that began on March 23, 1998. He chose to start his journey in Ghana as a way of rewarding the Ghanaians for being able to overcome their people's sad history of slavery and their nation's more recent political upheavals. The country's steps toward democratic government were being honored. The president spoke at Independence Square, and some older Ghanaians remembered that this was the same place where Queen Elizabeth II of the United Kingdom appeared when she made her state visit in 1961.

President Clinton made Ghana the first stop on his 1998 visit to Africa.

Enthusiastic crowds welcoming President Clinton

Although the president's visit to Ghana was brief, he received the warmest and most enthusiastic welcome of his entire trip there. Crowds lined the road leading from the airport. The crowd that came to hear him speak, estimated at half a million people, was both thrilled and honored by this visit. It was the first time in twenty years that a U.S. president who was still in office visited Africa. For that visit to begin in Ghana was an occasion for great celebration. He arrived at Kotoka International Airport to a traditional ceremony in which the spirits of the ancestors were called upon to witness and bless the occasion.

Peace Corps

Clinton's visit to a Peace Corps project was a reminder that Ghana was the destination for the first group of Peace Corps volunteers. They were sent by U.S. president John F. Kennedy in 1962. Today, the Peace Corps in Ghana is still one of the largest groups anywhere, numbering more than 150 people. Its main project centers around improving farming output. Working with a U.S. group called TechnoServe, the Peace Corps volunteers assist 175 communities across the country in improving their crop production and getting the crop to market.

The Peace Corps sends volunteers to communities across Ghana.

President Clinton was the most famous American to visit Ghana in recent years. In 1974–1976, Shirley Temple Black, a popular movie star of the 1930s, was named ambassador to Ghana by President Gerald Ford. In addition to these well-known Americans, many ordinary Americans go to Ghana for a quite different reason.

African-Americans

Ghana is a particularly important destination for African-Americans, descendants of Africans brought to America in chains. They go to find their own history. They look for some trace of their ancestry. They see the slave forts, they walk the same roads the slaves walked before their long, treacherous journey out of Africa, and they search the faces of the Ghanaians, hoping to make a personal connection. Most do not know where their ancestors were born. They only know that many Africans left Africa right at the place where President Clinton made his speech, in sight of the ocean that carried them away.

For one African-American, that connection came true. Her name is Maya Angelou, and she is well known today as an author and poet. When she went to Ghana in 1962, she had written only one book. Through the months that she lived

Maya Angelou

in Ghana, she struggled to find a place for herself. She was at once African and American, and eventually she came to realize that she was both. But still she searched for some connection with her eighteenth-century ancestors. And then, one day, just before she was scheduled to leave Ghana, she found that connection in a small town called Keta. There, right on the Atlantic Ocean, the slave trade had hit the Ewe village very hard. Virtually all the adults were taken away, leaving only children behind. The children watched as their parents were put into chains, never to be seen again.

Those children grew up in the homes of people who lived nearby and, through the generations, the story of how they lost their parents was told over and over again. Suddenly, into their little town came a woman who looked just like them but who said she was from America. And they realized that she was the living proof that at least some of their ancestors had survived that terrible journey.

Maya Angelou left Ghana a few days later, glad to be alive, glad that her people had survived the dreadful trip known as the middle passage. Her story can be read in her book *All God's Children Need Traveling Shoes*.

Healing the Past

In 1998, Emancipation Day was celebrated for the first time. During this week-long event, held from July 25 to August 2, people gathered at one of the former slave castles to mark the abolition of slavery. A remarkable part of the event was the reburial of Samuel Carson and a woman named Crystal, two

National Holidays

New Year's Day	January 1
Anniversary of the Inauguration of the Fourth Republic	January 7
Independence Day	March 6
Good Friday and Easter Monday	Date varies
Labor Day	May 1
Republic Day	July 1
National Farmers' Day	First Friday in December
Christmas	December 25
Boxing Day	December 26

slaves who died many years before in the United States and Jamaica. Their remains were reburied at Assin Manso, the place where the slave traders decided on the value of human beings offered for sale.

Eating Well

There is a lively debate among Ghanaians about which food could be called the national dish. It depends very much on whether you are Asante, Fanti, Ewe, or something else. One of the best-known dishes is fufu, a starchy food made of yams. Yams are an important part of the diet in Ghana. The yams are boiled, peeled, and then pounded into a sticky mixture. Fufu is quite difficult to make and requires a skillful hand. It's easier if two women do it together since it thickens and becomes very difficult to pound as it is cooked. Once it is cooked, it is eaten with one's fingers along with a dish of stew made with groundnuts (peanuts). Vegetables used in a stew might include eggplant, tomato, okra, and beans.

Oware

Throughout Africa, adults and children play a game in which markers are moved within cups or depressions. There are usually twelve or fourteen markers, but some versions use as many as thirty-two. The game is made by wood-carvers in Ghana and other countries and is known by many names: *kikogo, mankala, bao, ayo, nsolo,* and *wari* or *oware,* depending on the local language. The idea of the game is to transfer or move markers around small cups that are carved into the wooden board. The markers may be polished seeds, dried beans, or pebbles—whatever is available. Experienced players move the markers so quickly that it may be difficult for a casual observer to follow the game. As the players move, they keep count of the markers they pick up.

The boards are often carved with figures at one end, or with lids that have elegant designs. The game is popular in the way checkers is popular because it does not require much equipment—it can even be played by digging holes in the ground—and it can be played at any level of skill. Some see it as a kind of war game in which pieces are captured and the "enemy," the opposing player, is "killed." The game is thought to be several thousand years old. Ancient versions were carved into stones in Ghana. The Asante kings played the game on a golden board.

Phone Shops

There are very few homes with telephones in Ghana. People have to travel to use a telephone. Even in Accra, many people use the phones in a shop. These are not conventional phones, known as land lines. They are cellular phones. The technology has moved so quickly, it is easier to set up a cellular phone system in a developing African country than to lay cables and string lines to bring service to all regions. In the phone shop, the customer tells the manager the number to reach. After the customer finishes the call, the charges are figured for the time used.

For Ghana, the struggle to improve daily life continues. There is a tremendous amount of work to do before all the people have clean drinking water and a good education. Black Africa's first independent nation still has a long way to go, but the people have their strong traditions to call upon, to guide them through their lives.

This shop offers cellular phone and Internet services.

Timeline

Ghanaian History

Ancestors of today's Ghanaians move into the region.	1st–9th centuries
Portuguese establish a fort at Elmina as headquarters for the gold trade.	1482
First Dutch fort erected at Moree.	1612
Dutch capture the Portuguese forts at Elmina and Shama.	1637
British capture several Dutch forts.	1665
British become dominant on the Gold Coast and begin trading in slaves.	1665–1700
The Asante capital at Kumasi is founded.	1695
Slave trade continues. About 5,000 slaves are traded each year from the main British trading posts at Cape Coast and Anomabu.	1700–1800

World History

2500 B.C.	Egyptians build the Pyramids and Sphinx in Giza.
563 B.C.	Buddha is born in India.
A.D. 313	The Roman emperor Constantine recognizes Christianity.
610	The prophet Muhammad begins preaching a new religion called Islam.
1054	The Eastern (Orthodox) and Western (Roman) Churches break apart.
1066	William the Conqueror defeats the English in the Battle of Hastings.
1095	Pope Urban II proclaims the First Crusade.
1215	King John seals the Magna Carta.
1300s	The Renaissance begins in Italy.
1347	The Black Death sweeps through Europe.
1453	Ottoman Turks capture Constantinople, conquering the Byzantine Empire.
1492	Columbus arrives in North America.
1500s	The Reformation leads to the birth of Protestantism.
1776	The Declaration of Independence is signed.
1789	The French Revolution begins.

Ghanaian History

The Asante invade the coast; the Danish and the Dutch abandon their trading centers; the British parliament outlaws slavery.	**1807**
The British government takes control of its private trading companies, which were operating the Gold Coast settlements.	**1821**
The British declare the Gold Coast a Crown Colony. The British defeat the Asante and claim the southern provinces.	**1874**
Seat of colonial government moved from Cape Coast to Accra.	**1877**
The British establish protectorates over Asante and the northern territories.	**1898–1901**
Campaign for independence is launched by Kwame Nkrumah, who forms the Convention People's Party (CPP).	**1949**
Nkrumah becomes prime minister of Gold Coast.	**1952**
The coastal and inland territories together with British Togoland become independent as Ghana.	**1957**
Ghana is declared a republic; Kwame Nkrumah becomes president.	**1960**
Nkrumah is deposed in a coup led by General Joseph Ankrah.	**1966**
The army seizes power, the Constitution is suspended, and all political institutions are replaced by a National Redemption Council.	**1972**
Another coup puts Flight Lieutenant Jerry Rawlings in power. Ghana returns to civilian rule under Hilla Limann.	**1979**
Rawlings seizes power again; all political parties are banned.	**1981**
Voters approve a Constitution designed to make Ghana a democracy. Political parties, prohibited since 1981, are allowed. Rawlings is elected president.	**1992**
Rawlings is reelected president.	**1996**

World History

1865	The American Civil War ends.
1914	World War I breaks out.
1917	The Bolshevik Revolution brings Communism to Russia.
1929	Worldwide economic depression begins.
1939	World War II begins, following the German invasion of Poland.
1957	The Vietnam War starts.
1989	The Berlin Wall is torn down as Communism crumbles in Eastern Europe.
1996	Bill Clinton re-elected U.S. president.

Fast Facts

Official name:	Republic of Ghana
Capital:	Accra
Official language:	English
Major religion:	None

Black Star Square

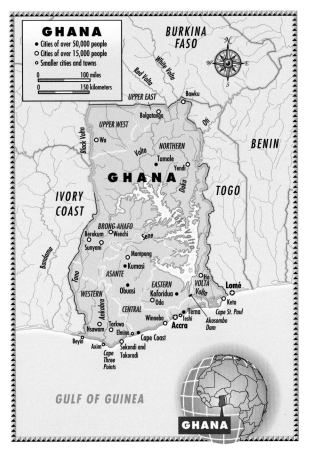

Ghanaian flag

Lake Volta

Children with homemade toys

Independence:	March 6, 1957 (from United Kingdom)
National anthem:	*Hail the Name of Ghana*
Government:	Constitutional democracy
Chief of state:	President
Head of government:	President
Area:	92,107 square miles (238,540 sq km)
Dimensions:	North-south, 418 miles (672 km) East-west, 335 miles (539 km)
Coordinates of geographic center:	8° 00' N, 2° 00' W
Bordering countries:	Ivory Coast (Côte d'Ivoire) is to the west, Burkina Faso is to the north, and Togo is on the east. The Atlantic Ocean lies to the south.
Highest elevation:	Mount Afadjato, 2,890 feet (881 m)
Lowest elevation:	Sea level
Climate:	Ghana's climate can be described as tropical. Temperatures generally approach 86°F (30°C) all year round, with greater humidity near the coast and in the forest regions. The north has cooler nights, but daytime temperatures often top those of the coastal region.
Average annual rainfall:	In the south, 50–83 inches (127–211 cm), concentrated in the spring and fall months. In the north, 43–50 inches (109–127 cm), concentrated in the spring and summer months.
National population (1998 est.):	18,497,206

Population of largest cities (est.):	Accra	1.6 million
	Kumasi	1 million
	Sekondi-Takoradi	300,000

Famous landmarks:

▶ ***Black Star Square*** (Independence Square) in Accra. Independence Day ceremonies every March 6 are held there.

▶ ***Osu Castle*** in Accra, also known as Christiansbourg Castle, has been the seat of government from 1876 to the present.

▶ ***Cape Coast Castle*** in Cape Coast stands on the site of the Swedish Fort Corolusbourg, built in 1653.

▶ ***Manhyia Palace*** in Kumasi is the home of the Asantehene. The National Cultural Center in Kumasi houses many items used by ancient Asante kings.

▶ ***Mole National Park*** in northern Ghana is the largest game reserve in the country.

Industry: Agriculture is at the heart of Ghana's economy. Cocoa is the most important crop, followed by cassava, plantains, and coco yams. Mining has become the most important source of foreign income, with gold the leading export, followed by diamonds, manganese, and bauxite. The principal industries are aluminum smelting, food processing, and lumber production.

Currency: The unit of currency is the cedi. In 1999, U.S.$1 = 2,495 cedi.

Weights and measures: Metric system

Literacy rate: 64.5% (males, 76%; females, 54%)

At work on a plantation

Currency

Forest and hills in the east

Jerry Rawlings

Common words and phrases:

Asantehene	Asante king
Adinkra	cloth printed with Asante symbols
chalay	friend
chao	plenty
coco	cornmeal porridge
durbar	festival
fufu	popular dish made of yams
Kente	handwoven Asante traditional cloth
ntama	a traditional garment
red red	fried plantain
smock	loose-fitting, handwoven cotton garment
tro tro	minibus used for traveling short distances

Famous Ghanaians:

Ama Ata Aidoo (1940–)
Writer

Kofi Annan (1938–)
UN secretary-general

Kwame Anthony Appiah
Writer

Kofi Awoonor
Writer

Kofi Abrefa Busia
Prime minister

Azumah Nelson (1958–)
Boxer

Kwame Nkrumah (1909–1972)
Independence leader and president

Jerry Rawlings (1947–)
President

Otumfuo Osei Tutu II
Asantehene

To Find Out More

Nonfiction

▶ Appiah, Kwame. *In My Father's House*. New York: Oxford University Press, 1992.

▶ Appiah, Peggy. *Tales of an Ashanti Father*. Illustrated by Mora Dickson. Boston: Beacon Press, 1989.

▶ Barnett, Jeanie M. *Ghana*. Let's Visit Places and Peoples of the World. Broomall, Pa.: Chelsea House, 1989.

▶ Department of Geography Staff. *Ghana in Pictures*. Visual Geography Series. Minneapolis: Lerner, 1988.

▶ *Ghana*. Major World Nations. Broomall, Pa.: Chelsea House, 1998.

▶ Levy, Patricia. *Ghana*. Cultures of the World. Tarrytown, N.Y.: Benchmark Books, 1999.

▶ Osseo-Asare, Fran. *Good Soup Attracts Chairs: A First African Cookbook for American Kids*. Gretna, La.: Pelican, 1993.

Websites

▶ **Ghana**

www.ghana.gov.gh
Includes a profile of the country and information on tourism, schools, news, culture and traditions, business opportunities, government, and sports.

▶ **Ghana Review International**

www.ghanareview.co.uk
The official website of GRI magazine includes sports, news, business and money, feature articles, art and culture, letters to the editor, and a section for young readers.

▶ **Republic of Ghana**

www.ghana.com/republic/index.html
The official website of Ghana includes information on history, presidents, currency, economy, regions, and festivals. Also includes links to maps, hotels, media, tourism, education, and job opportunities.

▶ **The World Factbook 1998**

www.cia.gov/cia/publications/fact-book/gh.html
This official CIA website lists facts on Ghana's geography, people, government, economy, transportation, communications, and transnational issues.

Embassy

▶ **Embassy of Ghana**

3512 International Drive, NW
Washington, DC 20008
(202) 686-4520
http://www.usembassy.org.gh/

Index

Page numbers in *italics* indicate illustrations.

A

Aboakyir festival, 113
abosom (Akan gods), 99
Accra, 16, 62–63, *63*, 119
    Black Star Square, 8
    electrical consumption of, 24
    map of, *63*
    population of, 83
    University at Legon, 53
Acheampong, Ignatius Kutu, 55
Adinkra cloth, 87–88, *88*, 105
Afram River, 25
African Company of Merchants, 41
African mahogany tree, 29
African-Americans, 123
agriculture, 24, *67*, 68–69, *68*, 72, 118
Aidoo, Ama Ata, 112, 133
Akan people, 82, 83, 93–94
Akoma symbols, 88
Akosombo Dam, 22–23, *23*, 53, 79
Akosombo Gorge, 20
Akuapem-Togo Mountain Ranges, 15–16
Akwambo festival, 111
Akyem people, 18
Akyempem cloth, 86
alluvial mining, 73
Angelou, Maya, 123–124, *123*
animal life
    antelope, 27, *27*
    birds, 28
    crocodiles, *26*, 27
    elephants, 27
    marabou, *28*

Ankobra River, 25
Annan, Kofi, 107, *107*, 133
antelope, 27, *27*
anthills, 29
Appiah, Kwame Anthony, 113, 133
archaeology, 33
Asante people, 18, 34–36, 40–46, *40*, 81, *82*, 99, 109
    Asantehene (king), 45
    British conquest of, 10, 44–45
    gold and, 40
    Golden Stool legend, 35, *35*, 45
    Kumasi and, 21, 42–43
Asante Uplands, 16
Ashanti Goldfields, 74, 79
Assin Attandanso Game Reserve, 30
Assin Manso, 125
Atlantic Ocean, 17, *17*
Awoonor, Kofi, 113, 133
Axim-Conga gold belt, 76

B

Bakatue festival, 110–111
baobab trees, 28, *29*
basketmaking, *81*
bauxite mining, 22–23
been-to people, 112
birds, 28
Birim River, 25
Black River, 22
Black, Shirley Temple, 123
"Black Star of Africa," 53
Black Star Square, 8

Black Stars (soccer team), 115
Black Volta river, 24
Boabeng Fiema Monkey Sanctuary, 27
Bobiri Forest Reserve, 27
Bomfobiri Wildlife Sanctuary, 27
borders, *14*, 15
Boti Falls, 27
boxing, 115
Brimati, Abhasan, *53*
British colonization map, *42*
Bronze Age, 33
buck. *See* antelope.
Burkina Faso, 15, 34
Busia, Kofi, 52, 54–55, 133
Busumtwe River, 21

C

cacao industry. *See* cocoa industry.
canopy walkway, 30, *31*
Cape Coast, *17*
Cape Coast Castle, *36*
cedi (currency), 74, *74*
chiefs, 60–61, *60*, 80
children, 92–93, *93*
Christianity, 101–102
cities
    Accra, 8, 16, 62–63, *63*, 119
    Keta, 124
    Kumasi, 21, 42–44, *42*, 119
    Sekondi, 21, 83
    Takoradi, 21, 78
    Tema, 21, 78, 83
climate, 19, 117
    Accra, 63
    cocoa industry and, 70
    flooding, 17
    Kumasi, 21
    northern savanna region, 18
    plant life and, 28
    Sekondi, 21
    Takoradi, 21
    Tema, 21

Clinton, Bill, 120, *120*
clothing, 81, 119
coastline, 16–17, *17*, 78
cocoa industry, 10, 13, *13*, 21, 53, 67–72, 68, *71*
    average annual production, 69
    British colony and, 47
    climate and, 70
Cocoa Marketing Board of Ghana, 69, 71
Cocoa Processing Company, 70
communications, 127, *127*
Constitution, 51, 57
Convention People's Party (CPP), 50
Côte d'Ivoire. *See* Ivory Coast.
crocodiles, *26*, 27
currency (cedi), 74, *74*

D

Daka River, 25
dance, 9, 108–109, *109*
Densu River, 25
Dipo-Krobo festival, 89–90
drums, *106*, 108
dzemawoi ("guardians of the worlds"), 99

E

economy, 51, 64
    cedi (currency), 74, *74*
    cocoa industry, 10, 13, *13*, 21, 53, 67–72, 68, *71*
    fishing industry, 76–78, *77*
    go-slow traders, 62
    gold industry, 10, 13, 21, *32*, *33*, 34, 66, 67, 73–76, *73*
    manufacturing, 72
    mining, 13, 72–73
    timber industry, 10, 76
    value-added tax (VAT), 78
education, 10, 47, 53, 96–97, *96*, *97*, 101–102
    Islamic schools, 103
    Kumasi University, 21, *21*

religion and, 101–102
University at Legon, 53
University College, 47
University of Cape Coast, 53
elections, 50, 57
electricity, 24, 78–79
elephants, 27
Elizabeth II, Queen of the United
    Kingdom, 120
Elmina Castle, 39, *39*, 41
Emancipation Day, 124
English language, 82–84
enstoolment, 35. *See also* Golden
    Stool.
erosion, 17
Ewe people, *16*, 52, 81–82, 83, 87, 109,
    109, 112, 124
executive branch (of government), 59

F
famous people, 133, *133. See also*
    people.
fantasy coffins, 105, *105*
Fante people, 41, 81
festivals, 110–113
fishing industry, 76–78, *77*
flooding, 17
foods, 64, *65*, 81, 118, 125
forests, *15*, 18, 29, 31, 68
fufu (food), *104*, 125
funerals, 98, 104–105

G
Ga people, 41, 81–82, 92, *111*, 112
Gbedema, Komla, 50
Gbelle Game Reserve, 27
General Electric Corporation, 79
geopolitical map, *11*
Ghana (Soninke kingdom), 33–34
Ghandi, Mohandas K. "Mahatma," 49

Ghartey IV, King of Winneba, 41–42
go-slow traders, 62
gold, 40, 88–89
Gold Coast, 9, 10, 34, 40, 42, *43*, 47
gold industry, 10, 13, 21, *32, 33*, 34, 66,
    67, *73*
    alluvial mining, 73
    Ashanti Goldfields, 74
    Obuasi gold mine, 73, *75*
    open-cast mining, 75
    proven gold reserves, 76
Golden Stool, 35, *35*, 45–46, 87
government
    chiefs, 60–61, *60, 80*
    Constitution, 51, 57
    Convention People's Party
        (CPP), 50
    elections, 50, 57
    executive branch, 59
    judicial branch, 58–59
    Legislative Assembly, 50
    legislative branch, 58, 59
    National Liberation Movement
        (NLM), 51
    parliament building, *57*
    prime minister, 50
    scientific socialism, 51–52
gun trade, 37
Gur language, 83
Gussiberg, Frederick Gordon, 47

H
hairstyles, 113, *113*
health care, 110
"highlife" music, 110
Hill, H. Worsley, 41
Hogbetsotso festival, 112
Homowo festival, 111–112,
    111
housing, 95–96, *95*

I

Independence Square, 120
insect life, 29
    mosquitoes, 44
    tsetse fly, 19
Islamic religion, 103, *103*
Ivory Coast, 15, 40

J

judicial branch (of government),
    58–59

K

Kakum National Park, 27, 30, *30*, *31*
Kente cloth, 85, *85*, 86
Keta, 124
King, Martin Luther Jr., 51
Kison, Albert, 22
Kotoka International Airport, 121
Kujani Game Reserve, 27
Kumasi, 21, 42–44, *42*, 119
    climate of, 21
    Manhyia Palace, 21
    population of, 21, 83
Kumasi Asanti Kotoko (soccer
    team), 21
Kumasi University, 21, *21*
Kwa language, 83
Kwawu people, 18
Kyeretwie cloth, 86

L

Lake Volta, 20, *20*, 22–24, *23*, 78, 79
languages, 82–84
    English, 84
    Gur, 83
    Kwa, 83
Legislative Assembly, 50
legislative branch (of government),
    58, 59

Limann, Hilla, 55
literature, 113
lost-wax casting, 89

M

Maclean, George, 41
Makola Market, 63–64, *64*
Mande people, 34
Manhyia Palace, 21
manufacturing, 72
maps
    Accra, 63
    British colonization, *42*
    geopolitical, *11*
    natural resources, 69
    population distribution, *84*
    slave trade, *38*
    topographical, *18*
marabou, *28*
marine life, 28, 76–78
markets, 63–65, 119, *119*
marriage ceremonies, 92
military, 54
millefiori beads, 89
mining, 13, 72–73
Mole National Park, 27, *27*
mosquitoes, 44
Mossi-Dagomba people, 82
Mount Afadjato, 15
music, *106*, 108

N

national anthem, 61
national coat of arms, 74
national flag, *61*, 62
national holidays, 125
National Liberation Movement
    (NLM), 51
National Theater, *62*
natural resources map, 69

Navrongo-Saboro region, 95
Nelson, Azumah, 115, *115*, 133
Nixon, Richard, 51, *51*
Nkrumah, Kwame, 12–13, *12*, 22, 49–54,
    50, *51*, *52*, 57–58, 133
Nmayem festival, 80
northern savanna region, 15, 18–19, *25*
Northern Territories, 46–47

O

Obuasi gold mine, 73, 75
open-cast mining, 75
Oti River, 25
outdooring ceremony, 91, 93
Owabi Bird Sanctuary, 27
Owabi Wildlife Sanctuary, 27
oware (board game), 126, *126*

P

Paga Crocodile Ponds, 27
Palm Sunday procession, *101*
Pan-African movement, 58
parliament building, *57*
Peace Corps, 122, *122*
people, 9, *54*, 65, 84, 96, 97, *100*, 106,
    108, *116*, *117*, *121*, *122*, *126*. See also
    Famous people.
    Akan, 82, 83, 93–94
    Akyem, 18
    Asante, 10, 18, 21, 34, 40–46, *40*, 81,
        82, 99, 109
    been-to, 112
    chiefs, 60–61, *60*, 80
    children, 92–93, *93*
    clothing, 81
    Ewe, *16*, 52, 81–82, 83, 87, 109, *109*,
        112, 124
    Fante, 41, 81
    funerals, 98, 104–105
    Ga, 41, 81–82, 92, *111*, 112
    hairstyles, 113, *113*
    health care, 110

housing, 95–96, *95*
    Kwawu, 18
    Mande, 34
    marriage ceremonies, 92
    Mossi-Dagomba, 82
    names, 84, 91
    oral history, 33
    polygamy, 94
    traditions, 104
plant life, *14*, *15*, 28–29
    African mahogany tree, 29
    anthills and, 29
    baobab trees, 28
    climate and, 28
    silk cotton trees, 29
    tropical forest zone, 18
    wawa tree, 29
plantations, 118
population, 67, 82
    Accra, 63
    distribution map, 84
    Kumasi, 21
    Sekondi, 21
    Takoradi, 21
    Tema, 21
Portuguese territory, 38
Positive Action program, 49
Pra River, 25
Pra River Basin, 70
Prempeh I, Asantehene of Asante
    people, 45, *45*
Prempeh II, Asantehene of Asante
    people, 46, *46*
priests, 101
prime minister, 50
proven gold reserves, 75–76
Pru River, 25

R

Rawlings, Jerry, 55, *55*, 56, 64–65, *65*,
    78, 133, *133*
religion, 99–100, *102*

Christianity, 101–102
    education and, 101–102
    Islam, 103, *103*
    Mande people, 34
    Palm Sunday procession, *101*
    priests, 101
reptilian life, 28, *28*
River Volta, 22
rivers, *22*, 24–25

S

Sankofa symbols, 88
Sao Jorge. *See* Elmina Castle.
scientific socialism, 51–52
Sekondi, 21, 83
Sene River, 25
silk cotton trees, 29
slave trade, 13, 36–37, *36*, 41, 89, 124
    Elmina Castle, 39, *39*
    gun trade and, 37
    map of, *38*
    trans-Saharan, 36–37
snakes, 28
soccer, *114*, 115
South Asante Uplands, 70
southern forestland region, 15
sports, *114*, 115
    Black Stars (soccer team), 115
    Kumasi Asanti Kotoko (soccer
        team), 21
St. George. *See* Elmina Castle.
strip weaving, 85–86, *86*

T

Takoradi, 21, 78
"talking drums," 108
Tano River, 25, 99
TechnoServe, 122
telephones, 127
Tema, 21
    harbor, 78
    population of, 83

timber industry, 10, 76
Togo, 15
topographical map, *18*
trade beads, *90*
trading beads, 89
traditional healers, 110
trans-Saharan slave trade, 36–37
transportation, 17, 25
tropical forest zone, 18
tsetse fly, 19
Tutu, Nana Osei, Asantehene of Asante
        people, 21, 35
Tutu, Otumfuo Osei II, Asantehene of
        Asante people, 91, 133
Tyrone-Grant, Kim, *115*

U

University at Legon, 53
University College, 47
University of Cape Coast, 53
upside-down tree. *See* baobab tree.

V

Valco Aluminum company, 24
value-added tax (VAT), 78
Volta Basin, 16, 47

W

Ware, Otumfuo Opuku II, Asantehene
        of Asante people, *10*, 91, *91*
wawa tree, 29
White River, 22, 24
wildlife. *See* animal life; insect life;
        marine life; plant life; reptilian life.
Wolseley, Sir Garnet, 44, *44*
World War II, 12, 48, *48*

Y

Yam festival, 110
yams, 125
al-Yaquiba, 33–34

Meet the Authors

ETTAGALE BLAUER is particularly intrigued by the culture of Ghana, especially the way it is expressed in material objects. The traditional method of weaving Kente cloth and the gold objects made for the Asantehene remind her of the long, continuous culture of the Ghanaian people. She admires the way people in West Africa dress in African garments and continue the traditions of their ancestors. She was fascinated by the proverbs of the Akan people and the way they are used in fabrics and other everyday objects. She is pictured at left with cloth and beads from Ghana.

JASON LAURÉ first visited West Africa in the early 1970s. Ghana is one of forty countries in Africa he has photographed. Each year he spends two to six months in Africa getting to know the people and the countries he visits. He considers the Ghanaian people to be the nicest and friendliest of all the people he has met in Africa. He particularly enjoys the bustling markets and admires the way women carry everything on their heads. He also found Ghana the most "African"—a country that has not been overwhelmed by cultures and products imported from Europe and the United States. He is pictured above in Teshi.

Photo Credits